Loaded with o[u]
activities fo[r]

Denver's Family Guide to Having Fun with Kids

2nd Edition

27 Brand *New* Delightful Destinations, more Restaurants and the improved Birthday Bash Directory

Justine M. Davros
Cindy Nead

SPECIAL BONUS: FIND OUT WHERE KIDS EAT FREE OR ALMOST FREE EVERY DAY OF THE WEEK!

FAMILY FUN 411

Denver's Family Guide to Having Fun with Kids

2nd EDITION

ISBN: 978-0-9841380-1-2

Illustrations by Can Stock Photo Inc. - Prawny

DEDICATION

Thanks to our husbands for believing in us, and to our children for inspiring us. We love you.

ACKNOWLEDGMENT

We are grateful to our mentors, advisors and friends who have provided the guidance, insight and support to help us accomplish this important venture in our lives. It is because of your collective knowledge, wisdom and willingness to share your vast experience that allowed this vision to become a reality.

TABLE OF CONTENTS

Adventure Golf and Raceway 11
Air Force Academy 11
AMC Theatres 12
American Mountaineering Museum 12
Arts on Fire 13
Bass Pro Shop 13
Boondocks Fun Center 14
The Broomfield Bay Aquatic Park................................... 15
Brunswick Zone 15
Buffalo Bill Museum and Grave...................................... 16
Build-A-Bear Workshop.. 17
Butterfly Pavilion... 18
Cave of the Winds 18
Cheyenne Mountain Zoo... 19
The Children's Museum of Denver 20
Chuck E. Cheese's 21
Colorado Adventure Park... 22
Colorado Avalanche Hockey Game.................................. 23
Colorado Avalanche Hockey Practice 23
Colorado Journey 24
Colorado Rapids.. 24
Colorado Rockies... 25
Colorado State Capitol 26
County Line BMX.. 27
Denver Aquarium 28
Denver Art Museum.. 28
Denver Center for the Performing Arts 29
Denver Firefighters Museum 30
Denver Museum of Nature & Science 30
Denver Nuggets Basketball... 31
Denver Puppet Theater 32
Denver Zoo 32
Dinosaur Ridge 33
Durango & Silverton Narrow Gauge Railroad.................... 34
Elitch Gardens 34
Fiske Planetarium and Science Center............................. 35
Fun City.. 36
Gateway Park Fun Center... 36
Georgetown Loop Train.. 37
Golf Zone Adventure... 38
Go Putt! Miniature Golf 38
Governor's Residence at The Boettcher Mansion............... 39

Hammond's Candies 39
Heritage Square 40
Home Depot (Kids Workshops) 40
House of Bounce 41
The Hudson Gardens & Events Center 41
Ice Skating at Copper 42
Ice Skating at Evergreen 43
Ice Skating at Keystone 43
Indoor Skydiving 44
Jack & Jill Children's Salon 45
Jo-Ann Fabric Superstore (Class Catalog) 46
Jump Street 46
Jungle Quest 47
Littleton Historical Museum 48
Lollilocks Kids Salon 48
Lowe's (Build and Grow Clinics) 49
The Makery 50
Michaels (The Knack Kid's Program) 50
The Molly Brown House Museum 51
Monkey Bizness 51
National Center for Atmospheric Research 52
National Oceanic Atmospheric Administration 52
Noah's Ark Animal Workshop 53
Peak Athletics Plus 53
Pirates Cove 54
Puppets and Things on Strings 55
Putter's Pride Mini Golf 55
Putting Edge Fun Center 56
Red Rocks Park 56
Royal Gorge Route Railroad 57
Skate City 57
Snip-Its 58
String Beads 58
Tiny Town 59
Town Hall Arts Center 60
Tubing at Copper Mtn. 60
Tubing at Keystone (Adventure Point) 61
Tubing at Keystone (Old Fashioned Family) 61
United States Mint 62
Water World 63
The Wildlife Experience 64
Wings Over the Rockies Air & Space Museum 64
Young Americans Center for Financial Education 65

FREE OR ALMOST FREE KID'S MEALS

Monday 69
Tuesday 74
Wednesday 82
Thursday.. 87
Friday 90
Saturday 93
Sunday 97

FREE ☺ OR ALMOST FREE KID'S MEALS BY
RESTAURANT 101
BIRTHDAY BASH DIRECTORY 🎁 102
FAMILY FUN BY COST FOR ADULTS 105

INTRODUCTION

The dreaded daily question from your young child, "So what are we going to do today?" This book was designed to help you easily answer that question. The Denver Metro area has many great things to offer, but we can't always think of things to do. Within these pages, we have provided many ideas to guide you towards fun and meaningful activities to do with your kids. Best of all, some of the activities are **free**. You may ask yourself why this book doesn't include a particular attraction. There are three reasons. Either we don't know about the attraction, it's an attraction that you will find in a future edition or it's not an attraction that we would recommend. It was our intention to stick to the excursions you are sure to enjoy.

You will find that this book is very informal and almost conversational. We wanted the information to be what you REALLY need to know and written as if your best friend was telling you about it.

HOW TO USE THIS BOOK

The contents of this book are listed alphabetically by attraction. The ages listed are simply our recommendations. While we have taken great care in making sure the information is correct, hours of operation and prices are constantly changing. The website of each attraction is your best source for the very latest information.

The **What to Expect** section is an overview of the attraction, while the **Notes/Tips** section will provide invaluable information that you need to know before you leave the house.

The following icons are used throughout the book to provide quick references: **$**, ☺ and 🎁.

$ indicates the general cost per adult for the attraction, unless adults cannot participate. Fees for children are often less. In the back of the book, you can find a list of attractions by cost.

$ Up to $10
$$ $10.01 to $15.00
$$$ $15.01 to $25.00
$$$$ more than $25.00

☺ indicates that the attraction is **free** for all ages. Activities not having a **$** or ☺ shown means that the cost varies.

🎁 next to an attraction indicates that they offer birthday party packages. We know that thinking of a creative place to have a birthday party can be a challenge. For a quick reference, you will find a list of birthday party locations in the back of the book.

Finally, we know that, inevitably, your excursion will include eating out. Therefore, near the end of the book we have included a list of restaurants (by day of the week), where kids eat **free** or almost **free**.

Enjoy the time with your kids and take all necessary safety precautions on each excursion.

ADVENTURE GOLF
AND RACEWAY $ 🎁

AGES 4+

9650 N. Sheridan Blvd.
Westminster, CO 80031
http://adventuregolfandraceway.com

303-650-7587

Hours: Seasonal - call for current hours

Cost for Golf: Kids under 4 **free**, Kids 4 – 12 $5.95, 13+ $7.95, Seniors 60+ $6.45.
Cost for Dragster drivers 48" or taller: $6.95
Cost for Raceway go-cart drivers 54" or taller: $5.75
Passengers are an additional charge

What to Expect: A 54-hole course full of unique experiences which includes a volcano, water and fire effects. In addition, the NASCAR themed raceway promises fast fun. The drag way simulates an actual race whereby you'll watch for the countdown to green to accelerate 0 – 60 in one second!

Notes/Tips: Although this course is priced higher than others, its attractions and features make it a worthwhile excursion. Visit website to download coupon.

AIR FORCE ACADEMY ☺

AGES 5+

2346 Academy Dr.
Colorado Springs, CO 80840
www.usafa.af.mil

719-333-2025
pa.comrel@usafa.af.mil

Hours: Daily 9 am to 5 pm

Cost: Free

What to Expect: The 31,600-square-foot Visitor Center contains exciting exhibits, concessions and a gift shop. A short movie showcasing the Academy can be viewed during your visit. In the exhibit area, you will find information about the Academy's history and learn about what it's like to be a cadet. Character development, academics, athletics, and military training are the four focus areas of the cadets.

Notes/Tips: To enter the Academy through the North Gate use Exit 156B on I-25 or use Exit 150 on I-25 for the South Gate. The Visitor Center, paved nature trail, and the Cadet Chapel do not allow backpacks or large bags. Go to the information desk for self-guided tour maps and information about the Academy. If you visit on a Wednesday or Friday, you may be able to watch the cadets marching to lunch at noon. Go to the Honor Court wall or the wall near the Cadet Chapel for the best view.

AMC THEATRES $ AGES 2+
www.amctheatres.com   888-262-4386
Enter your zip code at the top of the screen.

Hours: Vary - call or visit their website for show times

Cost: Kids under 2 **free**, Kids 2-12 yrs. $7, Adults $10, Seniors (60+) $9. 3D movies cost $3 more per ticket. All tickets ordered online are subject to a $1 service charge per ticket. Discounted tickets are available for shows before noon every day of the week.

What to Expect: A fun filled few hours with the family viewing the latest blockbuster hit.

Notes/Tips: Some theatres may offer $1 movies on early summer mornings. Call the theatre for details. Don't forget to bring extra money for concessions. Booster seats are available for the little visitors.

AMERICAN MOUNTAINEERING
MUSEUM $ 🎁   AGES 8+
710 10TH St.
Golden, CO 80401   303-996-2755
http://www.mountaineeringmuseum.org/
            info@mountaineeringmuseum.org

Hours: Mon. by appointment, Tues. – Fri. 10 am to 5 pm, Sat. 10 am to 6 pm, Sun. 11 am to 4 pm

Cost: Kids $4.50, Adults $6.50, Seniors $5

What to Expect: This museum recognizes famous mountaineers and provides education on the environment and culture related to the mountains. You will find exhibits, artifacts and lectures related to various famous mountain ranges.

Notes/Tips: Kids can test their skills on the climbing wall, but prearrangements are required through the Youth Education Program. For special offers text "Denver Mountaineering" to 32075.

ARTS ON FIRE 🎁   AGES 3+
9315 Dorchester St., #105
Highlands Ranch, CO 80129   303-470-0530
www.artsonfirestudio.com   artsonfirestudio@yahoo.com

Hours: Sun. - Wed. 11 am to 6 pm, Thurs. - Sat. 11 am to 8 pm. Other hours by appointment only.

Cost: Varies - depending on project

What to Expect: A fun and friendly paint your own pottery and glass-fusing studio. In a few easy steps, you will have created a one-of-a-kind masterpiece. The staff is incredibly helpful and will guide you every step of the way.

Notes/Tips: Check their website or call for the latest events and classes. All glazes are lead-free and all paints are non-toxic, which makes this place planet and family friendly. Your fired piece will be ready for pick up in one week.

BASS PRO SHOP ☺   AGES ALL
7970 Northfield Blvd.
Denver, CO 80238   720-385-3600
www.basspro.com select Denver Store
        Manager_Denver_CO@basspro.com

Hours: Mon. – Sat. 9 am – 10 pm, Sun. 10 am – 8 pm

Cost: Free

What to Expect: An outdoor lover's paradise. When a museum or aquarium just isn't in your budget, this store will certainly fill the void. It is far different than any other sporting goods store because it offers something for everyone to see and do. While browsing, you will view the fully stuffed Colorado wildlife throughout the store. You are also bound to stumble on the massive 21,000 gallon aquarium, with enormous fish that are fed every Saturday at 3:00 pm. For the daredevil, there is even a rock climbing wall and a shooting range laser game. Twenty-five shots will only cost you .50 cents.

Notes/Tips: Allow plenty of time to shop and experience all this store has to offer. Kids will love to waddle around with the live pet ducks. Friendly dogs are welcome too. Check out their website for events and **free** classes offered on the weekends. You may even want to eat at the in-store restaurant, Islamorada Fish Company.

BOONDOCKS FUN CENTER   AGES 4+
11425 Community Center Dr.
North Glen, CO 80233   720-977-8000
www.boondocksfuncenter.com

Hours: Sun. – Thurs. 10 am – 10 pm, Fri. and Sat. 10 am – Midnight. Check website for holiday hours.

Cost: Varies - depending on attraction

What to Expect: Family amusement center containing go carts, bumper boats, mini golf, batting cages, laser tag, flight simulator, arcade, a toddler play area and concession stand.

Notes/Tips: Check website for Tuesday specials. Kids can bring in their report cards with A's and B's receive tokens for the arcade. Lockers are available. Checks are not accepted. No outside food or drink is allowed in the facility and parking is free.

THE BROOMFIELD
BAY AQUATIC PARK $ 🎁   AGES 1-13
250 Lamar St.
Broomfield, CO 80020   303-464-5520
www.broomfield.org/recreation/bayinfo.shtml

Hours: Usually End of May thru Early Sept., Mon. - Thurs. 2 pm – 8 pm, Fri. 10 am – 8 pm, Sat. and Sun. 10 am – 6 pm

Cost: Kids 3 and under **free**, Kids 4 – 17 and Seniors 60+ $6, Adults $8, Residents receive a discount.

What to Expect: An interactive pool playground with a tot pool, 2 twisting water slides and a tube slide. The party room is outdoors with two tables.

Notes/Tips: Lockers are available. Padlocks can be purchased if necessary. Picnic tables can be reserved or covered tables are also available but on a first-come, first-served basis. There is a concession stand. It is ok to bring in your own food but not glass or alcohol. Visit the website for Friday Family Night specials. The fishing and swim with your dog events are annual and held at the end-of-season.

BRUNSWICK ZONE $ 🎁   AGES 3+
www.bowlbrunswick.com

2200 S. Peoria
Aurora, CO 80014   303-750-7045

1135 S. Wadsworth Blvd.
Lakewood, CO 80232   303-985-1578

945 S. Kipling Pkwy.
Lakewood, CO 80226   303-980-0300

9255 Kimmer Dr.
Lone Tree, CO 80124   303-792-2695

9150 Harland St.
Westminster, CO 80031   303-426-6352

9751 W. 49th Ave.
Wheat Ridge, CO 80033   303-425-1601

Hours: Vary - call or visit their website for open bowling times

Cost: Varies - depending on time and day. Approximately $.99 to $5 per game per person, but may vary by location. Plus cost of shoes - $1.99 kids' shoes, $3.79 adults' shoes. Call for the best price on day and time. Weekend prices are higher.

What to Expect: An enjoyable bowling experience in a smoke-free environment.

Notes/Tips: Sign up on their website to receive a **free** bowling coupon and other offers via e-mail.   Food is available for purchase. Don't forget to ask about the gutter bumpers for children. The maximum number of people per lane is six.   Brunswick Zone XL locations offer additional amenities such as laser tag and an arcade. You can expect one game for four people to take approximately 40 minutes.

BUFFALO BILL MUSEUM
AND GRAVE $ AGES ALL
987 ½ Lookout Mountain Rd.
Golden, CO 80401   303-526-0744
www.buffalobill.org   betsy.martinson@denvergov.org

Hours: Daily 9 am to 5 pm, May-Oct.; 9 am to 4 pm Tues. - Sun., Nov.-Apr.

Cost: Kids under 5 **free**, Kids 6-15 yrs. $1, Adults $5, Seniors (65+) $4; Only cash, checks or traveler's checks are accepted.

What to Expect: Here's a unique opportunity to go back in time to learn about Buffalo Bill's life, the times of the old west, view his grave and visit the museum.

Notes/Tips: Check out the website for more information about the latest exhibits. On the way to the museum, don't forget to stop and see the buffalo.

BUILD-A-BEAR WORKSHOP $$$ 🎁 AGES ALL
www.buildabear.com

Aspen Grove
7301 S. Santa Fe Dr.
Littleton, CO 80120   720-283-2327

Cherry Creek Shopping Center
3000 E. 1st Ave, Ste. 191
Denver, CO 80206   303-320-9888

Colorado Mills
14500 W. Colfax Ave.
Lakewood, CO 80401   303-216-9700

Flatiron Crossing
1 W. Flatiron Crossing Dr.
Broomfield, CO 80021   720-887-9001

Hours: Mon. - Sat. 10 am to 9 pm and Sun. 11 am to 6 pm

Cost: $20 (estimated cost based on what is chosen)

What to Expect: A stuffed animal workshop.

Notes/Tips: Your children will love making a furry friend by stuffing it, placing a heart inside and personalizing a birth certificate. If your child loves stuffed animals, this place is sure to be a hit. Adorable accessories are available such as: tees, boxers, hats, bags and lots of cool stuff for as little as $2 - $10. If that isn't enough, there are hundreds of outfits available. One visit to Build-A-Bear Workshop and your child will be hooked!

BUTTERFLY PAVILION $ 🎁   AGES ALL

6252 W. 104th Ave.
Westminster, CO 80020   303-469-5441
www.butterflies.org   marketing@butterflies.org

Hours: Open Daily, 9 am to 5 pm; must enter 45 minutes before closing. Closed Thanksgiving Day and Christmas Day.

Cost: Kids under 1 yr. **free**, Kids 2–12 yrs. $5.50, Adults $8.50, Seniors (65+) $6.50

What to Expect: An interactive place for adults and kids alike to learn about insects, butterflies, sea creatures, turtles and more. You are sure to enjoy seeing many beautiful butterflies up close.

Notes/Tips: The average visit is 1.5 hours with kids. Parking is free and the tables outside are great for picnicking. If you wear comfortable shoes, you can end your day with a short .5 mile nature hike with the kids. Check the calendar online for exciting "bug" events. Busy times for school groups are generally Mon. through Fri. 10 am to 1 pm, Sept. through May.

CAVE OF THE WINDS   AGES ALL

100 Cave of the Winds Rd.
Manitou Springs, CO 80829   719-685-5444
www.caveofthewinds.com

Hours: Vary – call or visit website. Open 364 days a year.

Cost: Varies depending on tour selected. Military discounts may apply. Fees apply for tickets purchased online.

What to Expect: An exciting exploration event, which will take you into a new underground adventure to learn about cave formation and its natural creatures. A visitor center, gift shop, and seasonal snack bar are available on site.

Notes/Tips: Caves are not wheelchair accessible. Strollers and baby backpacks (unless worn in front) are not allowed. You will be ready for your cave experience with your camera, comfortable shoes, clothes that can get dirty and a light jacket. Parking is free.

CHEYENNE MOUNTAIN ZOO $$ 🎁   AGES ALL

4250 Cheyenne Mountain Zoo Rd.
Colorado Springs, CO 80906   719-633-9925
www.cmzoo.org   info@cmzoo.org

Hours: The Zoo is open 9 am – 6 pm Memorial Day weekend through Labor Day and is open 9 am – 5 pm all other times of year. See their website for holiday and special events hours.

Cost: Kids 2 and under **free**, Kids 3–11 $7.25, Adults $14.25, Seniors $12.25. Groups of 15 people or more receive a discounted admission.

What to Expect: A 3-acre exhibit called Rocky Mountain WILD! This zoo is America's only mountain zoo; which means it is uniquely suited to show Colorado wildlife in its natural setting. The Rocky Mountain Wild exhibit will draw you to the highest and most spectacular part of the Zoo.
Here you experience surprising, engaging and memorable encounters with Rocky Mountain wildlife. Be prepared to see the moose, lynx, mountain lion, grizzly bear, river otter and bald eagle. Animals will appear to roam freely  on the side of Cheyenne Mountain, as the exhibit is designed to skillfully enclose the animals' natural habitat.

The indoor aviary exhibit, Budgie Buddies is fun for kids of all ages. Everyone will love to be surrounded by hundreds of free-flight birds and enjoy offering the birds a snack.

Mountaineer Sky Ride will enable you to view popular zoo exhibits from the air. This chairlift ride will take to you to the overview where you can also see the breathtaking view, have the kids enjoy the specially designed playground or grab a bite to eat or refreshments. Ride hours vary.

Your family can also enjoy pony rides, the carousel, the tot train, the tram, and My Big Backyard, which is a nature-themed playground. This exhibit encourages kids to use their imaginations. The playground includes an animal contact area for hands-on opportunities while romping and playing.

Notes/Tips: Don't miss hand feeding the giraffes! This just might your child's highlight of the day. Giraffe crackers are available for purchase. Be sure to check out the special shows throughout the zoo. Check the schedule for your favorite creature's show. You will see the zoo keepers interact and feed the animals.

There are gently sloped walking paths throughout the Zoo. Remember, the zoo is on a mountain so be sure to wear your most comfortable footwear. Strollers are available to rent. The zoo offers camps for kids that are filled with adventures that entertain and educate. They do not accept out-of-state personal checks. See their website for coupons!

Outdoor seating is located at many locations around the Zoo for picnic eating. Picnic/sack lunches are allowed. Don't forget to stop at the gift shop and snack bar before heading home.

THE CHILDREN'S MUSEUM
OF DENVER $ 📱

AGES 0-8

2121 Children's Museum Dr.
Denver, CO 80211
www.mychildsmuseum.org

303-433-7444
information@cmdenver.org

Hours: Mon. – Fri. 9 am to 4 pm, Weds. open until 7:30 pm, Sat. and Sun. 10 am to 5 pm

Cost: Infants **free**, Age 1 $6, Ages 2–59 $8, Seniors (60+) $6.

What to Expect: An interactive place of discovery designed to capture a child's mind and imagination, as well as engage them physically. This place is built for kids with a variety of climbing structures and a special area for infants. The other museum attractions include: a mini grocery store, a craft center, a workshop where your child can build using real tools and recycled household materials. A kid-sized basketball court, a train center, and a stage for dancing, singing, acting or putting on a puppet show is also available. Aspiring veterinarians have a special exhibit too.

Notes/Tips: Expect to spend at least two hours to see all the museum has to offer. There is a gift shop and a café to grab a snack or lunch. Because field trips are not allowed on Mondays, this is a great day to explore the museum.

CHUCK E. CHEESE'S 📱   AGES ALL
www.chuckecheese.com

9301 Ralston Rd.
Arvada, CO 80002   303-425-5925

14005 E. Exposition Ave.
Aurora, CO 80012   303-340-5855

1001 W. Hampden Ave.
Englewood, CO 80110   303-761-8636

7510 Parkway Dr.
Littleton, CO 80124   303-706-1155

305 Marshall Rd.
Superior, CO 80027   720-304-8814

Hours: Vary by location

Cost: Varies

What to Expect: An indoor amusement center with interactive video games, toddler rides, Skee-Ball and play structures. The main dining room may have attractions like video dancing and animatronics. Tickets are earned for prizes. Families can enjoy a variety of pizza and salad menu items.

Notes/Tips: Plan extra time for your child to trade tickets for prizes, which can easily take 15 minutes or more. Saturdays tend to be especially busy, crowded and loud. It can be difficult to keep track of kids during the busy times. For coupons, see their website or the Sunday paper.

COLORADO ADVENTURE PARK 🎁 AGES 2+

566 County Road 721
Fraser, CO 80442   970-726-5779
www.coloradoadventurepark.com
                    info@coloradoadventurepark.com

Hours: 10 am – 10 pm. Mid Nov. – Mid Apr.

Cost: Varies – depending on activity chosen

What to Expect: A winter park with a variety of winter activities for everyone including sleigh rides, tubing, airboarding, sledding and snow mobiles for kids 6 years and up to 130 pounds. A surface lift will transport you back up to the top of the hill.

Notes/Tips: We highly recommend you call for reservations and current snow conditions. Dress head-to-toe in warm, waterproof clothing and don't forget goggles or sunglasses, sunscreen and lip balm. Helmets are required and can be rented if needed. Concessions and free Wi-Fi are available in the warming hut. Save time and download the waiver form before you go. Tubing participants must be 3 years or older. Sledding is **free** for kids 3 and under. Personal checks are not accepted.

COLORADO AVALANCHE
HOCKEY GAME $$$$ AGES ALL
Pepsi Center - 1000 Chopper Cir.
Denver, CO 80204   Tickethorse: 866-461-6556
http://avalanche.nhl.com/

Hours: Vary - depending on game you choose

Cost: Seats start around $28

What to Expect: A professional hockey game with lots of hits and crowd pleasing excitement.

Notes/Tips: Check the website for family nights, which includes food and reduced ticket prices (minimum four tickets). Food can be expensive, so consider eating before you leave. Expect to pay for parking. Light rail is also an option. See website for additional information, including: practices, player statistics, team standing, schedule of player appearances around town and so much more.

COLORADO AVALANCHE
HOCKEY PRACTICE ☺   AGES ALL
Family Sports Center
6901 S. Peoria St.
Englewood, CO 80112   303-708-9500

Hours: Non-game days, while they are in town. Call for exact time.

Cost: Free

What to Expect: A professional hockey practice with up-close viewing of fast skating and maybe even a phony fight.

Notes/Tips: As an added bonus to your excursion, you may even be able to get an autograph or two if you wait by the motorized gate on the west side of the building after practice. Please be aware that all practice times and places are subject to change. We highly recommend calling Family Sports Center to confirm practice times or for additional information.

COLORADO JOURNEY $ 🎁   AGES 2+

5150 S. Windermere
Littleton, CO 80120   303-734-1083
www.sspr.org click on facilities/parks tab   aaronf@ssprd.org

Hours: Vary- see website or call

Cost: Kids under 5 yrs. free with paying adult, Youth/Senior $5.50, Adults $6.25, discounts apply for South Suburban district residents.

What to Expect: A Colorado themed miniature golf course with many fun structures to play through. The course is beautifully landscaped, with a little stream running alongside many of the holes. Each hole features a part of Colorado's interesting history. Even the score card contains some facts about each Colorado point of interest.

Notes/Tips: You are sure to enjoy this outing with your family. The facility offers free parking, a snack bar, nice picnic tables and wheelchair accessibility. On a hot day, the shade is limited on the courses. You'll be glad you brought sunscreen and a water bottle. It is easier to keep track of everything (golf ball, score card, pencil, water bottle, etc.) if you wear clothing with a lot of pockets. Purses tend to get in the way while you are golfing. Generally, it takes approximately 45 minutes to get through the course. This time will be extended if the courses are busy.

COLORADO RAPIDS $$$ 🎁   AGES ALL

Dick's Sporting Goods Park
6000 Victory Way
Commerce City, CO 80022   303-727-3500
www.coloradorapids.com   info@dsqpark.com

Hours: Check the website for game schedule

Cost: Varies depending on seats but usually start around $16. Tickets can be purchased online, in person at any Dick's Sporting Goods or by calling TicketHorse at 1-866-461-6556.

What to Expect: A major league soccer game in the biggest and most state-of-the art professional stadium and field complex in the world.

Notes/Tips: 32 oz. or less clear plastic water bottles are allowed. No outside food or other beverages are permitted. Dick's Sporting Goods Park is located at the intersection on 60th and Quebec Streets. There are three entrances to the park. Check their website for your best route. Website also contains great info on player appearances and special kids' programs. Parking is free.

COLORADO ROCKIES $ 🎁

AGES ALL

Coors Field
2001 Blake St.
Denver, CO 80205
www.coloradorockies.com

Main: 303-292-0200
Tickets: 303-ROCKIES or
800-388-ROCK

Hours: Vary – call or visit their website

Cost: $4 - $75+, game tickets are not needed for lap children two and under. No service charge for tickets purchased at the Coors Field ticket office. Expect to pay for parking.

What to Expect: Food, fun and baseball at one of America's most beautiful stadiums. In addition, the interactive kid's zone (located behind the bullpens near Gate A) boasts a video batting cage, tee-ball and throwing areas. A playground built especially for little kids is also available.

Notes/Tips: The Colorado Rockies thought of everything. They even have a family section (lower section of 342) in the stadium that does not allow alcohol. Booster seats can be checked out at Guest Relations behind Section 112.

Diaper changing stations are available in all men, women and family restrooms. Buckaroos (Section 149) is a special concession stand for kids. Healthy food choices can also be found throughout the park.

Camcorders and cameras are not allowed to record the game, but may be brought into the park. You can bring in your own food, but check the website for the latest restrictions. Glass bottles and cans are not allowed.

Batting practice (BP) occurs two hours prior to the games. However, most teams choose not to take BP on Sunday afternoon games. Check the website for autograph opportunities prior to home games.

If you really want to see the dugout, visitor's clubhouse, Press Level, Club Level, Suite Level and the Concourse area, check out one of the Coors Field tours.

Birthday parties are available before Sunday home games. Call 303-312-2444 to make reservations. Check out the Rockies Rookie Fan Club for a variety of baseball cool stuff for kids 15 and under.

The Colorado Rockies has a Designated Driver Program. See website for details to receive a free non-alcoholic beverage during the game.

COLORADO STATE CAPITOL ☺   AGES 7+

200 E. Colfax Ave.
Room 029, State Capitol
Denver, CO 80203   303-866-2604
http://www.colorado.gov/capitoltour
                    Simon.Maghakyan@state.co.us

Tour Hours: Aug. – May Mon. - Fri., 9:15 am to 2:30 pm and June – July. Mon. - Fri., 9 am to 3:30 pm. The Capitol is closed for most legal holidays.

Cost: Free

What to Expect: To be educated on Colorado's history, the Capitol construction, the legislative process, the gold dome, presidential portraits and a quick view of the law maker's offices. Historical tours are 45 minutes long and offered every 45 minutes and every 30 minutes in June and July. (Call 303-866-3834 for separate Capitol Dome and legislative tour information.)

Notes/Tips: Reservations are required for group tours. If you plan to make the 99 step tour to the top of the building, reservations are required. Call to be sure public tours are available for your visit. Parking can be expensive and difficult to find. Public transportation is a good option. Enhance your Capitol area experience by visiting other nearby attractions such as: the Governor's Mansion, U.S. Mint, Colorado History Museum and the Molly Brown House. Each attraction is within a 15 minute walk.

COUNTY LINE BMX ☺ 📖   AGES 6+
8560 S. Colorado Blvd.
Centennial, CO 80126   303-798-7515
www.ssprd.org click on facilities/parks tab   303-483-7017

Hours: Daily 8 am to dusk weather permitting.

Cost: **Free** on non-race days.

What to Expect: A bicycle moto-cross track.

Notes/Tips: For race information, refer to the website. Riders are strongly encouraged to wear a helmet, long pants, long sleeved shirt and enclosed shoes. Bikes should also have a padded cross-bar. There is no concession stand at the track and no shade. Seating is very limited, so bring your own. Call the weather hotline at 303-483-7017 for specific information pertaining to the track. Birthday parties here are an unforgettable blast!

DENVER AQUARIUM $$    AGES ALL

700 Water St.
Denver, CO 80211   303-561-4450
www.aquariumrestaurants.com   Click on Denver website

Hours: Sun. – Thurs. 10 am to 9 pm, Fri. & Sat. 10 am to 9:30 pm

Cost: Kids 2 and under **free**, Kids 3–11 yrs. $9.25, Adults 12 – 64 yrs. $14.95, Seniors (65+) $13.95.   4D theater ticket $4.95.   After 6:00 pm admission discounts and free parking may apply if you choose to dine at the restaurant. Otherwise, there is an additional charge for parking.

What to Expect: To learn about different creatures that live in the following habitats: the desert, the sea, the wharf, the rain forest, the coral lagoon and the beach. Don't miss the seven minute 4D movie simulating an underwater experience.

Notes/Tips: Dining at the restaurant can be costly and it is recommended only for older kids. Allow at least an hour and a half to walk through and see the aquatic life, reptiles and tigers. A snack bar and gift shop are available. Special programs include: Marine Biologist for a day, Zoologist for a Day, overnights and camps.   Reservations for groups are required two weeks in advance.

DENVER ART MUSEUM $ AGES 8+

100 W. 14th Ave. Pkwy.
Denver, CO 80204   720-865-5000
www.denverartmuseum.org

Hours: Vary – call or visit their website.   Closed on Mondays.

Cost: Kids 5 and under **free**, Kids 6–18 yrs. $3, Adults $10, Seniors (65+) and College Students $8. Out of state visitor admission costs are slightly higher. **Free** admission on the first Saturday of every month for Colorado residents. Service charges do not apply if you buy your tickets on site. Some exhibits are an additional cost.

What to Expect: A wonderful learning journey into various types of cultural arts such as: African, American Indian, Asian and oceanic. Interesting lectures and films are offered at various times. Most tours are **free** with admission. This museum has been recognized internationally for its pleasant family atmosphere.

Notes/Tips: Parking is available in the garage at 12th and Broadway. Remind your party that the "no touch rule" applies to the artwork. Free lockers are available. Food and drinks are only allowed in designated areas. Families are welcome to checkout a museum backpack, which contains art supplies, games and puzzles. For shorter visits, ask for an art tube to make your own art activity. Don't forget to check out the Fun Family Center and Kid's Corner, where you can play dress up and create more art. Check their website for kid's classes and summer camps.

DENVER CENTER FOR THE PERFORMING ARTS   AGES 6+
1101 13th St.   303-893-4000
Denver, CO 80204   Tickets: 303-893-4100
www.denvercenter.org   feedback@dcpa.org

Hours: Vary – check event calendar on website for show times

Cost: Varies - depending on show

What to Expect: A live theatre experience, which hosts nationally known plays in an award-winning atmosphere. Many aspiring actors train here.

Notes/Tips: Student matinee tickets may include a post-performance discussion with members of the company. To enhance your theatre excursion, your children might enjoy riding the Light Rail downtown. Light Rail stops across the street from the facility. Our recommended dress code at most performances is church attire.

DENVER FIREFIGHTERS MUSEUM $ 👜

AGES ALL

1326 Tremont Pl.
Denver, CO 80204   303-892-1436
http://www.denverfirefightersmuseum.org
                    info@denverfirefightersmuseum.org

Hours: Mon. – Sat. 10 am to 4 pm

Cost: Kids 1-12 yrs. $4, Adults $6, Seniors and Students $5

What to Expect: An exciting opportunity for kids and adults alike to learn about Denver's Firefighting history, equipment and fire safety. Kids can watch videos, slide down an actual fire pole, dress up in firefighting equipment and climb on a real fire truck.

Notes/Tips: Bags larger than 11" x 15" are not allowed past the self-service check area. It is recommended that you leave all bags in your car. This is one of the best kept secrets in Denver, especially for birthday parties. It's affordable, with an enormous fun factor.

DENVER MUSEUM OF NATURE & SCIENCE ☺ 👜

AGES 3+

2001 Colorado Blvd.
Denver, CO 80205   303-370-6000
www.dmns.org   feedback@dmns.org

Hours: Mon. - Sun. 9 am to 5 pm except Christmas day. Check their website for exhibit hours.

Cost: Varies – depending on attraction

What to Expect: A relaxed science education center that includes: exhibits, programs and activities to learn about our state, planet and the universe at large. You will experience a museum, IMAX theater, planetarium, snack bar, café, gift shop, library and Discovery Zone for kids.

Notes/Tips: Visit their website for **free** days available to Colorado residents. A fee still applies to IMAX and Planetarium shows. Active members of the military and their spouses/partners and children receive **free** Museum admission (separate fee still applies to IMAX, Planetarium, and temporary exhibitions). If you arrive after 5:00 pm for an IMAX film Fri. and Sat., tickets must be purchased at the ticket window inside the east entrance to Phipps IMAX Theater starting at 5:30 pm. Long lines often form on weekends and holidays. Plan to arrive an hour before an IMAX film or Planetarium show is scheduled to begin to ensure enough time for parking and purchasing tickets. Tickets may be purchased in advance. Check their website for several children's workshops and family activities. Families will need at least five hours to experience all the museum has to offer. It is well worth your time.

DENVER NUGGETS
BASKETBALL $$ AGES ALL
Pepsi Center
1000 Chopper Cir.
Denver, CO 80204   303-405-1100
www.nba.com/nuggets   nuggetsmail@pepsicenter.com
Tickets: www.nuggetsseats.com

Hours: Check the website for game schedule.

Cost: Varies - depending on seats but adult tickets with fees start around $15. Kids under 2 **free**.

What to Expect: A fun-filled evening enjoying America's professional basketball players in action.

Notes/Tips: Visit their website for promotions, fun theme nights and **free** kid's games. No outside food, drinks or cameras allowed.

DENVER PUPPET THEATER $ 📖   AGES 3-7

3156 W. 38th Ave.
Denver, CO 80211   303-458-6446
www.denverpuppettheater.com   annie@hypermall.net

Hours: Vary- call or visit their website

Cost: $7 per person

What to Expect: A lively show with marionettes and audience participation. Children can make their own craft, while they wait for the show to begin.

Notes/Tips: Doors open 30 minutes before show time. Kids can play with a variety of puppets before and after the show. We don't recommend the show for kids over seven years old. The shows change about every three months. Parking is very limited, so arrive early.

DENVER ZOO ☺ 📖   AGES ALL

2300 Steele St.
Denver, CO 80205   303-376-4800
www.denverzoo.org   zooinfo@denverzoo.org
This website is also available in Spanish.

Hours: Vary – call or visit their website. Admission gates close at 5:00 pm in the summer and at 4:00 pm in the winter.

Cost: Varies – call or visit their website. Check their website for **free** days.

What to Expect: Exciting animals from all areas of the world including mammals, fish, amphibians, birds and invertebrates (species which have bones or cartilage). There is a carousel, a train (additional charges apply) and interesting animal facts. Count on an entire day of walking.

Notes/Tips: Parking is free. Purchase discounted tickets at your local King Soopers Stores, Rockies Dugout Stores or at TicketsWest.com. There are concession stands but picnic lunches are allowed. However, glass containers or alcohol are not permitted. Baby Strollers, Wagons, Motorized Wheel Chairs and Adult Pushchairs are available for rent. Plan your visit around the various feeding times. These demonstrations are a must see. Call the zoo or visit their website for the schedules. For a small fee, you can ride the safari shuttle that tours the Zoo paths at regular intervals. From early Dec. through early Jan. go see Zoo Lights where over 35 acres are illuminated with millions of dancing lights which makes for a fun holiday family event. Visits are especially nice in the spring so that you can see the baby animals. The zoo offers education programs for families, schools and communities.

DINOSAUR RIDGE ☺ 🎁   AGES ALL

16831 W. Alameda Pkwy.
Morrison, CO 80465   303-697-3466
www.dinoridge.org   tours@dinoridge.org

Hours: The ridge is open sunrise to sunset. The visitor center hours vary depending on the season.

Cost: Free but donations are welcome. Guided tours - $3 per person with several weeks advanced reservations only. A $36 deposit is also required.

What to Expect: A dinosaur experience where you will see and learn about fossils, tracks and preservation.

Notes/Tips: Dinosaur Ridge is an adventure for all ages. You'll want to bring hiking shoes, water, snacks for the kids, a camera and don't forget the binoculars. Picnic tables are available. If this is your first visit, we recommend stopping by the visitor center and gift shop. Check their website for special events.

You can either experience the Dinosaur Ridge Trail (1.5 mile hike) on foot or for an additional fee ride the shuttle bus.

How about turning your children and their friends into Paleontologists for the day? Dinosaur Ridge offers birthday parties! Kids will get to dig and find dinosaur bones. This is recommended for Paleontologists six to ten years of age.

DURANGO & SILVERTON NARROW GAUGE RAILROAD   AGES ALL

479 Main Ave.   877-872-4607
Durango, CO 81301   970-247-2733
www.durangotrain.com

Hours: Vary – call or visit their website

Cost: Varies - depending on attraction

What to Expect: A spectacular journey on board a vintage steam locomotive. While traveling along the Animas River from Durango to Silverton, you can relive the sights and sounds of yesteryear.

Notes/Tips: Families can board the train in Durango or Silverton. However, if you take the train from Silverton, you will need to stay the night in Durango. The ride can be very long. We recommend taking the train one way and the bus the other way. See the website for special events. Previous events have included: The Polar Express, Santa Reception in the Depot, Pumpkin Patch Express and Day out with Thomas.

ELITCH GARDENS $$$$ 🎁   AGES 1+

2000 Elitch Cir.
Denver, CO 80204      303-595-4386
www.elitchgardens.com   info@elitchgardens.com

Hours: Vary, April to October. Please see website or call ahead. Island Kingdom Water Park is open 10 am to 6pm Memorial Day to Labor Day.

Cost: 3 and under **free**, Under 48" $29.99, 48" and taller $40.99. Online price- Under 48" $27.99, 48" and taller $38.99. Note- processing fees apply when purchasing tickets online. Call and ask about coupon promotions at local retailers.

What to Expect: An exciting amusement park and water park adventure.

Notes/Tips: Early birds are rewarded by being at the gates when they open because the crowds tend to be FAR less in the morning. Also, April, May, June and September tend to be less crowded. Weekdays during the summer can be a good time to visit as well. Check website for special event days.

Consider taking the light rail to avoid the parking fee. If you plan to visit more than once a year, look into a season pass early in the season. As you might expect, Elitch Gardens has 13 rides for the younger kids and plenty of rides for the older kids.

Outside food is not permitted in the park, but you can bring in clear water bottles. If you are planning on a full day of sun and fun, don't underestimate the amount of snacks and drinks you will need stocked in your car. You can come and go to your car as often as you like. You will save a TON of money by going back to the car for a picnic lunch.

There is plenty of fun in the sun at Island Kingdom Water Park. Free life jackets are available at the raft rentals. The water park is included in your general admission ticket.

FISKE PLANETARIUM AND SCIENCE CENTER $ 🎁

AGES 4+

2414 Regent Dr. (University of Colorado)
Boulder, CO 80302
http://fiske.colorado.edu

303-492-5002
fiske@colorado.edu

Hours: Mon. - Fri. 8:30 am to 4 pm

Cost: Kids $3.50, Adults $7, Seniors $3.50, Students $5

What to Expect: An exciting place for all to learn about the planets and universe through live talks, concerts, laser shows and much more.

Notes/Tips: Check their website for the schedule of music shows and parking options. High school, community college and university students are **free** for all Thursday night live talks. Student identification cards are required.

FUN CITY 📷   AGES 4+
9670 W. Coal Mine Ave.
Littleton, CO 80123   303-972-4344
http://funcitycolorado.com

Hours: Vary – call or visit their website

Cost: Varies - depending on attraction

What to Expect: A family entertainment center, which includes: Grand Prix Raceway, laser tag, bowling, miniature golf, a virtual battle in a simulator pod, arcade, inflatables, the Twister ride, foam ball play room, rock climbing wall, a little town for kids 10 and under, bar and restaurant.

Notes/Tips: Discounted passes are available at King Soopers, Safeway and TicketsWest. We found that the all day passes are the way to go if you have several hours to enjoy all Fun City has to offer. Holidays at Fun City are insanely busy.

GATEWAY PARK FUN CENTER 📷   AGES 2+
4800 No. 28th St.
Boulder, CO 80301   303-442-4386
www.gatewayfunpark.com   events@gatewayfunpark.com

Hours: Summer Hours – Daily 10 am – 11 pm. See website for other seasonal hours.

Cost: Varies – depending on attraction

What to Expect: An indoor and outdoor family amusement center containing miniature golf, go-kart track, kiddie karts, kiddie land, human maze, batting cages, arcade and snack bar.

Notes/Tips: Outside drinks and any other food with the exception of pizza and outside drinks are allowed. There is a covered picnic area.

GEORGETOWN LOOP TRAIN $$$ AGES ALL
646 Loop Dr.
Georgetown, CO 80444   303-569-0147
or   Toll Free Reservations 888-456-6777
845 Railroad Ave.
Silver Plume, CO 80476
www.georgetownlooprr.com

info@historicrailadventures.com

The Georgetown Loop Historic Mining and Railroad Park is located 45 miles west of Denver, just off Interstate 70. Visitors may board the train at either the Devil's Gate Station (Exit 228) in Georgetown or the Silver Plume Depot (Exit #226).

Hours: Vary - call or visit their website

Cost: Kids 3 and under **free** when sitting on an adult's lap, Kids 4 + $16.50, Adults $22.50

What to Expect: A beautiful ride on a locomotive through the old mining towns of Georgetown and Silver Plume. You and your family will travel 7 miles round trip on gauge track, while viewing Colorado's spectacular scenery. During your ride, visitors can also tour the Lebanon Silver Mine.

Notes/Tips: Reservations are recommended. You may purchase tickets online or onsite. Car seats and strollers are not permitted on the train. Check the website for special events to add something special to your family outing. The train cars are open. Be sure to dress for the mountain weather. Kids- don't forget to watch for wildlife during your visit. Mule deer have been spotted in the area. On site gift shops offer snacks and drinks.

GOLF ZONE ADVENTURE $ 🎁   AGES 3+

18442 Pony Express Dr.
Parker, CO 80134   303-805-7005
www.golfzoneadventure.com

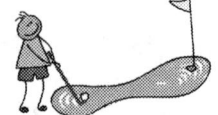

Hours: Vary – call or visit their website

Cost: Kids under 3 **free**, Kids 3 – 10 $4, Kids 11 – 18 $5, Adults $6, Seniors $5

What to Expect: Two 18-hole mini-golf courses with multi-leveled obstacles and water features. A large outdoor seating area for parties is available.

Notes/Tips: On Monday nights, an 18-hole round is discounted and includes a serving of free popcorn. If you get those afternoon munchies, Golf Zone has just the snack bar for you.

GO PUTT! MINIATURE GOLF $ 🎁   AGES 3+

9741 Park Meadows Dr.
Lone Tree, CO 80124   303-768-0096
www.goputtminigolf.com   goputtcolorado@aol.com

Hours: Open every day - weather permitting. Closed on Thanksgiving and Christmas.

Cost: Kids under 3 **free**, Kids 3 – 9 $5.50, Adults/Youth Ages 10+ $7.25

What to Expect: Putters playful mini golf course with features such as waterfalls, streams and tricky but fun holes. A safe, clean and fun activity for all ages.

Notes/Tips: Stroller and wheelchair friendly. Checks are not accepted.

GOVERNOR'S RESIDENCE AT
THE BOETTCHER MANSION ☺ 　　AGES 8+

400 E. 8th Ave. 　　　　　　　　303-866-5344
Denver, CO 80203
www.colorado.gov/governor/mansion/index.html

Hours: Call for tour hours

Cost: Free

What to Expect: A tour of the governor's residence, which was built in 1908 and contains several historical artifacts.

Notes/Tips: No reservations are required. Parking is available on the corner of 8th Avenue and Logan Street.

HAMMOND'S CANDIES ☺ 🎁 　　AGES ALL

5735 N. Washington St.
Denver, CO 80216 　　　　　　　303-333-5588
www.hammondscandies.com

Hours: Tours every 30 minutes Mon. - Fri. 9 am to 3 pm and Sat. 10 am to 3 pm., Sun. Closed

Cost: Free

What to Expect: *Cavities and hyper children (just kidding).* An interesting and fun place to learn about the candy making process.

Notes/Tips: No reservations necessary for groups under ten. The factory uses peanuts and other allergen causing products. Bring money for the candy store.

HERITAGE SQUARE $$$ 🎁   AGES ALL

18301 W. Colfax Ave.
Golden, CO 80401   303-727-8437
www.heritagesquare.info
www.heritagesquareamusementpark.com
info@heritagesquareamusementpark.com

Hours: Vary, please see website or call ahead. Rides open seasonally.

Cost: Free to get in, rides are an additional cost. You can pay per attraction or purchase an unlimited pass for the rides. The Alpine Slide and train ride is not included in the unlimited pass.

What to Expect: An amusement park, fishing, miniature golf, magic show, theatre and shopping. Check the website for special events.

Notes/Tips: Nestled in the foothills of Golden, Heritage Square is a great place for all ages. Because general admission is free, you can bring the grandparents to watch the kids have fun. Parking is free too! We certainly like that parents can ride free on eight rides with their children. You can bring in your own food and dine at the free family picnic area. The online videos will give you a great idea of what to expect at the park. Don't forget to sign up online for the e-newsletters and coupons will be sent to you.

HOME DEPOT
(Kids Workshops) ☺   AGES 5-12

www.homedepot.com*   (800)HomeDepot

Hours: First Saturday of the month between 9 am and 12 pm. Call your nearest store for the class times.

Cost: Free

What to Expect: Quality one-on-one time with your child, while completing an educational and practical take home project with real tools. Home Depot staff will provide tool safety tips and instruction. Your child will receive a Home Depot apron and a special project pin.

Notes/Tips: Kids' workshops are offered at all Home Depot stores. *Go to their website and enter Kids Workshop in the search box to find out about upcoming projects. Project kits are limited, so arrive on time. Parents should expect to assist with the project. Don't forget your camera to capture your little carpenter in action!

HOUSE OF BOUNCE $ 🎁   AGES 2-10
8000 S. Lincoln St. #4
Littleton, CO 80122   720-283-2899
www.houseofbounce.net   info@houseofbounce.net

Hours: Vary - based on season, call or visit their website

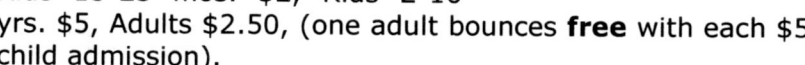

Cost: Kids under 12 mos. **free**, Kids 13-23 mos. $2, Kids 2-10 yrs. $5, Adults $2.50, (one adult bounces **free** with each $5 child admission).

What to Expect: Bouncy indoor inflatable fun for children.

Notes/Tips: Socks are required, but they can be purchased on site. Parents can watch from the viewing areas. Children over 11 are not allowed to bounce. Concessions are not available, but outside food is allowed in the lobby.

THE HUDSON GARDENS
& EVENTS CENTER $ AGES ALL
6115 S. Santa Fe Dr.
Littleton, CO 80120   303-797-8565
www.hudsongardens.org   info@hudsongarden.org

Hours: Daily 9 am – 5 pm. May thru Oct.

Cost: Kids under 3 **free**, Kids 3 – 12 $2, Adults $5, Seniors 60+ $3, Military $1

What to Expect: A mile and a quarter walk through thirty acres of beautiful gardens, ponds and sculptures. One can expect to see frogs, fowl, feathers, flowers, vegetables, a garden railroad, and a variety of shaded coves.

Notes/Tips: November thru April are contribution months and guests can decide on their own admission cost. Take advantage of the free family explorer packs which has activities to learn about leaves, frogs, bees, trees as well as your own senses. Guided tours require a 72-hour advanced reservation. Golf cart tours are offered to a maximum of five guests. Check the website for concert schedule, classes and events. Picnics are welcome.

ICE SKATING AT COPPER ☺   AGES 2+

West Lake
Copper Mountain, CO 80443   970-968-4info
www.experiencecopper.com Click on search and ice skating
(Access to this website is not available in the off-season.)

Hours: Daily 10 am to 9 pm

Cost: Admission is **free**. Skate Rentals: $10

What to Expect: An outdoor skating, broomball or curling adventure, while enjoying the breathtaking mountain scenery.

Notes/Tips: Couple the above activities with the s'mores kit available at the Rocky Mountain Chocolate Factory (Copper One Lodge) and you'll have a definite family bonding experience.

ICE SKATING AT EVERGREEN $ AGES 3+

29614 Upper Bear Creek Rd.
Evergreen, CO 80437   720-880-1300
Skating hotline (updated daily)   720-880-1391
www.evergreenrecreation.com   Click   on   facilities   and
Evergreen Lake House link
(Access to this website is not available in the off-season.)

Hours: Varies, please see website or call ahead after mid November.

Cost: Kids under 3 **free**, Kids 3-12 yrs. $4.50, Kids 13-18 yrs. $4.75, Adults $5, Seniors (55+) $4.50; skate rental $6 for 2 hours, $3 for each additional hour. Cash or checks only. No ATM available on site.

What to Expect: A frosty fun day with the family. Hockey, broomball and other skating activities make it a great time for all. If you get chilly, take a break in the warming house with hot chocolate and other goodies.

Notes/Tips: Parking is limited, so look for shuttle service during peak hours. Hockey sticks and pucks cannot be rented. This is a favorite family excursion in the mountains at an affordable price.

ICE SKATING AT KEYSTONE $$ AGES 2+

Lakeside Village
22101 US Highway 6
Keystone, CO 80435   970-496-7103
http://keystone.snow.com/info/winter.iceskating.asp
(Access to this website is not available in the off-season.)

Hours: Usually 9 am – 10 pm Dec. – Mar. weather permitting. Check the website.

Cost: Kids under 12 yrs. $7 + Skate Rental $4, Kids 12–17 yrs. $9 + Skate Rental $5, Adults $11 + Skate Rental $7.

What to Expect: North America's biggest, cleanest and smoothest outdoor skating rink manicured by an ice resurfacer. Besides traditional ice skating, your hockey player can partake in some good ole pick up pond hockey. Your ice skating experience will be complemented with a beautiful backdrop of lights and music.

Notes/Tips: Free glow sticks and necklaces are given to children on Mondays. What to wear: layers, layers, layers & sun protection. Hockey equipment is not provided. Don't break your back teaching your child to skate. Skate walkers are available for kids and adults! Check out the lake webcam on the photos and videos website tab to see current ice conditions. In addition, we highly recommend you also call Keystone ice rink to speak to a staff representative about whether or not sticks and pucks will be allowed on the day you plan to go. Park in the Keystone Conference Center lot, which is across the highway from Lakeside Village.

INDOOR SKYDIVING $$$$ 🎁   AGES 4+

9230 Park Meadows Dr.
Lone Tree, CO 80124   303-768-9000
www.skyventurecolorado.com

Hours: Open 9 am daily

Cost: Children under 12 yrs. $43, Adults $48. Check website for package deals.

What to expect: A five story building in a wind tunnel with 1200 horsepower fans that recreates the feeling of actually skydiving. Beginners and experts will NOT forget this experience.

Notes/Tips: Reservations are recommended but walk-ins are accepted. Arrive 45 minutes prior to flight time for registration and safety training. Everyone flies with an instructor. Each person gets 2 one-minute rotations in the tunnel. The observation area is almost as entertaining as the indoor skydiving itself. If you want to capture this momentous occasion on video, you may want to consider buying the DVD that Sky Venture offers. Although, the footage will not record your skydiver higher than two feet above the glass, at least it will be better than you shooting *through* the glass. Indoor skydiving is a great gift for the adventurous person and we give it a high thrill factor.

JACK & JILL
CHILDREN'S SALON 🎁   AGES 1–12
www.jackandjillchildrenssalon.com

14605 E. Arapahoe Rd.
Aurora, CO 80016   303-364-0050

Hours: Mon. – Fri. 9 am to 6 pm, Sat. 9 am to 5 pm, Sun. 10 am to 3 pm

222 Milwaukee St.
Denver, CO 80206   303-780-0050

Hours: Mon. – Fri. 9 am to 6 pm, Sat. 9 am to 5 pm, Sun. 11 am to 4 pm

9233 Park Meadows Dr.
Lone Tree, CO 80124   303-347-0050

Hours: Mon. – Fri. 9 am to 6 pm, Sat. 9 am to 5 pm, Sun. 10 am to 3 pm

Cost: Varies - depending on service

What to Expect: A fun salon offering supreme kid-friendly services such as haircuts, hairstyles, ear piercing, manicures and pedicures. Your child can even sit in a special character chair, while being pampered.

Notes/Tips: Appointments are recommended. Here's a super place to have a birthday party for your little diva! There are plenty of party themes to choose from and your daughter will never forget the year she celebrated in salon style.

JO-ANN FABRIC SUPERSTORE
(Class Catalog) $$$$ 📖   AGES 5+
www.joannfabrics.com - Search for class catalog

7360 S. Gartrell Rd.
Aurora, CO 80016   303-690-5281

9090 E. Phillips Pl.
Centennial, CO 80112   303-799-1741

6795 W. 88th Ave.
Westminster, CO 80031   303-431-9300

Hours: Class times vary. Call or visit website to inquire about class times.

Cost: Depending on project, the cost ranges from approximately $35 – $65.

What to Expect: Classes such as quilting, sewing, candy making, jewelry making, t-shirt art, knitting, watercolor, crochet and flower arrangement.

Notes/Tips: Reservations are required for the classes. Supplies are not included in the cost of the classes. Free demonstrations are available on Saturdays.

JUMP STREET 📖   AGES 18 Mos.+
www.gotjump.com

10081 W. Bowles Ave.
Littleton, CO 80127   303-339-3030

8225 North Valley Hwy.
Thornton, CO 80221   303-426-5867

Hours: Sun. – Mon. 11 am – 9 pm, Tues. – Thurs. 10 am – 10 pm and Fri. – Sat. 10 am – 12 am (midnight)

Cost: Varies – depending on attraction

What to Expect: Indoor trampoline park with an open jump area, dodge ball arena, arcade, batting cages (in Thornton) and inflatable castles and slides for younger children. Guaranteed, your child will be exhausted when he leaves.

Notes/Tips: All jumpers must fill out a waiver. Save time and download a waiver before going. At the Littleton location, there is a great coffee shop with free Wi-Fi where parents can sit, relax or watch TV while the kids bounce and run around. No outside food or drink is allowed.

JUNGLE QUEST $$ 📱
www.junglequest.net

AGES 5-12

8000 S. Lincoln St., Ste. 10
Littleton, CO 80122

303-738-9844
explore@junglequest.net

Hours: Mon. – Sat. 9 am to 6 pm, after hours and Sunday reservations available

Cost: Mon. – Thurs. $11 for 1.5 hrs, Fri. & Sat. $12 for 1.5 hrs

9499 Washington St.
Thornton, CO 80229

303-920-9404
explorethornton@junglequest.net

Hours: Vary- call or visit their website

Cost: $15 for 1.5 hrs.

What to Expect: A child's version of mountain climbing on rock walls. Other fun includes: a tree house, bridges, zip lines, and tunnels. Sorry, no climbing for parents but you can watch from the lookout area.

Notes/Tips: Space is limited and reservations are recommended. Friendly safety instructors are on hand to tame the jungle enthusiasts. Children should wear comfortable clothing for climbing. Camps are also available in the summer.

LITTLETON HISTORICAL MUSEUM ☺

AGES 4-12

6028 S. Gallup St.
Littleton, CO 80120
www.littletongov.org/museum

303-795-3950

Hours: Tues. – Fri. 8 am to 5 pm, Sat. 10 am to 5 pm, Sun. 1 pm to 5 pm, closed Mondays and holidays

Cost: Free

What to Expect: An education on the history, art and culture of Littleton, Colorado. While roaming the 39 acres of the museum, you will see two living history farms, a lake, a collection center and a main exhibit building. A tour guide will explain what it was like to work on a farm and complete jobs like blacksmithing and sheep shearing.

Notes/Tips: Groups should call for information on scheduling and fees. History camps are offered for kids entering fourth, fifth and sixth grade. Closed shoes are a good idea since the grounds are unpaved. During the annual harvest event, there are several fall activities for the kids like the pumpkin patch. You'll be glad you brought your own wagon to transport your pumpkins. Since this is a popular event, parking is brutal. Be ready to walk.

LOLLILOCKS KIDS SALON 🎁

AGES 1-12

www.lollilocks.com

2525 Arapahoe Ave.
Boulder, CO 80302

303-442-5654
boulder@lollilocks.com

9358 Dorchester
Highlands Ranch, CO 80129

303-683-5007
highlandsranch@lollilocks.com

Hours: Vary- call for information

Cost: Varies – depending on service

What to Expect: Expert stylists will work their magic to create the latest hair-do, while making your child feel special. A manicure and/or ear piercing can accentuate the pleasurable experience.

Notes/Tips: Appointments can also be made online! Salon parties include themes like rock star, Luau and princess. All theme parties include a salon service, a craft, entertainment and a favor. This is an excellent party idea for your girly girl!

LOWE'S
(Build and Grow Clinics) ☺   AGES 5-12
www.lowes.com*   800-44-Lowes

Hours: Twice a month 10 am to 11 am. Call or visit the website.

Cost: Free

What to Expect: A fun-filled kid's workshop activity such as a periscope, mini golf game and keepsake box. This is a great bonding experience for you and your child.

Notes/Tips: *To register online for a clinic, go to the website. Type Build and Grow into the search box, and then follow the instructions to sign up and complete the waiver. Kid-size tools are used for the project. Your child will receive an apron and a patch. A high level of parental participation is required. When we attended, we were surprised to find a $10 gift card included, since the project was right before Mother's Day.

THE MAKERY $$$    AGES 3+

8203 S. Holly St.
Centennial, CO 80122
www.themakery.com

720-270-4042
info@themakery.com

Hours: Vary - call or visit their website for class schedule

Cost: Varies - depending on class or party

What to Expect: To make, bake and decorate your own cake. Here's the best part - your kitchen stays clean!

Notes/Tips: Children's parties start at around $20 per person, plus a $20 per hour instructor/room fee. You must sign up for a class or party to participate.

MICHAELS
(The Knack Kid's Program) ☺ 📖   AGES 5-12

www.theknackkids.com   800-michaels

Hours: Check your local store for free events on scheduled Saturdays and exact class times.

Cost: Free

What to Expect: An enjoyable morning with your child, while creating an artistic craft together. Your child may discover new skills and build confidence through their project.

Notes/Tips: Check the website for the craft schedule and classes. There may even be a **free** activity offered.

THE MOLLY BROWN
HOUSE MUSEUM $

AGES 8+

1340 Pennsylvania St.
Denver, CO 80203
303-832-4092
www.mollybrown.org

Hours: Vary – call or visit their website

Cost: Kids 5 and under **free**, Kids 6-12 yrs. $4, Ages 13-64 yrs. $8, Seniors (65+) $6

What to Expect: A story about an amazing woman, who survived the most famous and fascinating sinking ship, The Titanic. When you visit her home, you will get a sense of her upper class Victorian lifestyle.

Notes/Tips: Visit their website for special exhibits and events, which require a reservation. Parking is available east of the museum at 13th Avenue and Pearl Street. Food is not available at the museum, but there are plenty of restaurants nearby.

MONKEY BIZNESS $ 📱

AGES 1+

9950 E. Easter Ave., Ste. 200
Centennial, CO 80112
303-790-8885
www.monkeybizness.com
info@monkeybizness.com

Hours: Mon. – Fri. 9 am to 6 pm (open until 8 pm on Weds.)

Cost: Kids 12-23 mos. $3, Ages 2+ yrs. $7.50, Adults are free for open play.

What to Expect: An indoor playground consisting of interactive inflatables, a climbing wall, play structures and a separate area for toddlers.

Notes/Tips: Socks are required. The rock wall is only available to children attending a party. All children must be supervised by a parent during open playtimes. Free Wi-Fi is available. Feel free to bring a sack lunch or a snack and use the party rooms during open play time.

NATIONAL CENTER FOR ATMOSPHERIC RESEARCH ☺   AGES 5+

1850 Table Mesa Dr.
Boulder, CO 80305   303-497-1174
www.ncar.ucar.edu

Hours: Mon. – Fri. 8 am to 5 pm, weekends and holidays 9 am to 4 pm

Cost: Free

What to Expect: This is a great hands-on educational field trip for everyone to learn about the atmosphere and similar sciences. A nature preserve and wildlife range is also on site for enjoyment.

Notes/Tips: Guided tours are available at noon daily and take approximately one hour.

NATIONAL OCEANIC ATMOSPHERIC ADMINISTRATION ☺   AGES 5+

325 Broadway   Tour Reservations: 303-497-4091
Boulder, CO 80305   Tour Info: 303-497-3333
www.esrl.noaa.gov/outreach/tours.html

Hours: Tues. at 1 pm ONLY

Cost: Free

What to Expect: Several learning opportunities while visiting the weather operations center, the science on a sphere and other research divisions. Tours take about 90 minutes.

Notes/Tips: Visitors should first call the tour information line for the latest security procedures. Plan to bring a US photo ID or foreign passport and allow plenty of time to get through security to make it to your tour by 1:00 pm. Tour reservations are required.

NOAH'S ARK ANIMAL WORKSHOP $$$$ 🎁

AGES 3-7

4731 W. 136th St.
Crestwood, IL 60445
www.noahsarkworkshop.com

866-484-6624

custservice@noahsarkworkshop.com

Hours: Mon. – Fri. 9 am to 5 pm CST

Cost: $26 Average (excludes shipping)

What to Expect: Your house to become a furry friend workshop. You order the kit(s) to create your own animal(s) or purse. You can also request a party hostess.

Notes/Tips: You can invite Mojo Monkey to attend party or event. Upon receipt of your kit, you will hand-stuff your own animal, name it, dress it and create a birth certificate. You can add sound and other accessories at an additional cost. Price based on parental willpower.

PEAK ATHLETICS $$$$ 🎁   AGES 3+

399 Dad Clark Dr.
Highlands Ranch, CO 80126
www.peakathleticsplus.com

303-797-8082

Hours: Vary - depending on parent's night out or class taken

Cost: $30/child for parent's night out (members receive a discount)

What to Expect: A parent's night out two Saturdays a month from 6 pm to 10 pm. During the four hours of fun, kids will enjoy games, open gym, crafts and a movie. Dinner is also included. You can expect a tired child upon your return. The kid's gym also offers gymnastics, cheerleading and dance classes for children 3 years and up.

Notes/Tips: Kids attending the parent's night out must be potty trained. Special programming exists for boys.

PIRATES COVE $ 🎁      AGES 2+

1225 W. Belleview Ave.
Englewood, CO 80120   303-762-2683
www.piratescovecolorado.com   pirates@englewoodgov.org

Hours: Open from Memorial Day through Labor Day 10:30 am to 6:30 pm. They are only open weekends from last part of August through Labor Day.

Cost: Kids 2-17 yrs. $8, Adults 18-54 yrs. $9.25, Seniors 55+ yrs. $8. Discounts available with Englewood or South Suburban ID card.

What to Expect: A family water park with a lazy river, leisure pool with a play structure, water slides, sand play area, competitive pool and a spray garden.

Notes/Tips: On hot days, plan to arrive a half an hour before the rides open. This will allow you plenty of time to get a great spot for the day. Small coolers and picnics are allowed. You will also find many food choices on site. Children must be at least 48" tall to ride the slides. The maroon slide is the fastest one and it's reserved for the swimmers who are brave enough to withstand the four second in-the-dark ride. The open orange slide is the slowest and the yellow slide is a medium speed with lots of twists and turns. Don't forget to visit the lazy river. This is a wonderful way to relax and cool off.

Pirates Cove is one of the most affordable small water parks in the Denver area. You just can't beat the price for the size of the park. There is also a peace of mind that comes with knowing that your kids are within a three minute walk to every attraction. Keep in mind, the park will not be open if the weather forecast is 65 degrees or less.

PUPPETS AND THINGS
ON STRINGS 🎁 AGES 4+
The Star Theatre
8800 S. Colorado Blvd.
Highlands Ranch, CO 80126 303-771-3154
www.ventmarkshows.com ventmark@aol.com

Hours: Vary - with scheduled party

Cost: $125 for Basic Party Package

What to Expect: A puppet and ventriloquist show that contains giggles and audience interaction combined with storytelling. Some of the featured entertainment includes programs titled: 'Health and Fitness', 'Adventure in Reading' and 'Adventure in Ventriloquism'.

Notes/Tips: If you are looking for a birthday party to entertain and captivate the kids, this is the show for you. Celebrate your child's birthday at your home or at the theatre. Most shows are an hour long. Adults will appreciate the talent it takes to put on such a show.

PUTTER'S PRIDE MINI GOLF $ 🎁 AGES 3+
3604 S. Kipling St.
Lakewood, CO 80235 303-985-3860
www.putterspride.com

Hours: Vary – call or visit their website

Cost: Kids under 12 $4.50, 13 + $7, Seniors 60+ $4.50

What to Expect: A stroll through as many as 54 holes of miniature golf while enjoying the sights and sounds of the wildlife, flowers, goldfish pond and ghost town.

Notes/Tips: There is a picnic area and large lawn for the kids to frolic.

PUTTING EDGE FUN CENTER $ 🎁   AGES 3+
Colorado Mills Shopping Center
14500 W. Colfax Ave. Ste. 337
Lakewood, CO 80401   303-202-0260
www.putting-edge.com   coloradomills@puttingedge.com

Hours: Mon. – Fri. 11 am to 9 pm,
Sat. 10 am to 9 pm, Sun. 11 am to
6 pm. Call for holiday hours.

Cost: Kids under 5 **free** with adult
or senior admission, Kids 5-6 yrs. $6.50, Kids 7–12 yrs.
$7.50, Adults $8.50, Seniors $6.50

What to Expect: Indoor miniature golf in psychedelic style
with an arcade.

Notes/Tips: This is a nice rainy day activity and kids love
the glow in the dark aspect of this experience.

RED ROCKS PARK ☺   AGES ALL
18300 W. Alameda Pkwy.
Morrison, CO 80465   303-697-4939 or 303-295-4444
www.redrocksonline.com

Hours: 5am to 11pm

Cost: Free

What to Expect: Beautiful scenery overlooking the Denver
skyline, a visitor center, a 1.4 mile hiking trail through
magnificent rock formations, a picnic area and
amphitheatre.

Notes/Tips: Check to be sure there are no events
scheduled on that day (e.g. concerts). The annual Easter
sunrise service is a favorite event of the locals. This is
clearly one of the best places in the country to see a
concert.

ROYAL GORGE
ROUTE RAILROAD

AGES ALL

401 Water St.
Canon City, CO 81212
www.royalgorgeroute.com

888-724-5748

Hours: Vary- please see website or call ahead

Cost: Varies depending on the package you choose

What to Expect: A wonderful train ride through the beautiful Royal Gorge, while traveling next to the Arkansas River.

Notes/Tips: There are a variety of ride packages to review. It is important to book early. The Santa Express train ride is extremely popular during the holiday season. Children can wear their favorite pajamas and drink hot chocolate during this early evening ride. Santa's elves will be busy reading holiday stories to the children, while you are enjoying tranquil ride through the mountains. Be sure to have your list ready for Santa when he enters the train.

SKATE CITY $ 🎁

AGES 3+

www.skatecitycolorado.com

15100 E. Girard Ave.
Aurora, CO 80014

303-690-1444

5801 S. Lowell Way
Littleton, CO 80123

303-795-6109

200 W. 121st Ave.
Westminster, CO 80234

303-457-0220

Hours: Vary - call or visit their website

Cost: $4.50 for two hours. There are also special fun sessions ranging from $3.50 - $6. Skate rental is an extra fee.

What to Expect: A roller rink playing the most popular hits, as well as the classic group favorites like YMCA, The Hokey Pokey, etc. Roller contests such as fast skate and limbo are also held. Skating classes and inline hockey leagues are held at each location.

Notes/Tips: Lockers are available. The birthday party child receives a new pair of skates. Traditional roller skates, speed skates and inline skates can be used and rented. Free Wi-Fi is available.

SNIP-ITS $$$$ 🎁   AGES 1-6
11290 Twenty Mile Rd.
Parker, CO 80134   720-851-SNIP
www.snipits.com

Hours: Mon. – Sat. 9 am to 6 pm, Sun. 10 am to 4 pm

Cost: Varies - depending on depending on party package)

What to Expect: An opportunity for your daughter and her friends to make believe they are going to a Hollywood red carpet event or just having fun dressing up glamorously. Blooming beauticians may also choose to practice on a Snip-Its doll.

Notes/Tips: The Dashing Diva party director will handle all of the fun so parents can relax. Cake, juice and party favors are included, as well as a gift for the birthday girl.

STRING BEADS $ 🎁   AGES 3+
9555 S. University Blvd. #103
Highlands Ranch, CO 80126   720-344-3419
www.stringbeadsinc.com

Hours: Mon. - Sat. 10 am to 6 pm, except Wed. 10 am to 8 pm, Sun. 12 pm to 5 pm

Cost: $10 (average) or more depending on your selections

What to Expect: A full service bead store where you can choose from a wide variety of beads and charms. Then, design and string your own creations. An associate will complete your projects by securing the ends of your jewelry, so you can take your beautiful finished pieces home that day.

Notes/Tips: There are books, tools and stringing supplies to purchase also. Classes are offered, along with parties for any occasion. This is a fun place to take kids (even boys) to make your own jewelry. Allow at least half an hour to complete your project. The more beads you add, the more your project will cost.

TINY TOWN $  AGES 1-5
6249 S. Turkey Creek Rd.
Tiny Town, CO 80465   303-697-6829
www.tinytownrailroad.com

Hours: Memorial Day through Labor Day daily 10 am to 5 pm; Open weekends during May and Sept. 10 am to 5 pm

Cost: Kids under 2 **free**, Kids 2-12 yrs $3, Adults $5. Train fare is $1 per person.

What to Expect: A child's size village with a miniature steam railroad for visitors to ride. Children and adults alike can explore 90 playhouses like structures with doors large enough to accommodate little adventurers.

Notes/Tips: This quaint little town is built among one of Colorado's most beautiful canyons. Families can enjoy the picnic area and playground. Due to the dirt terrain, a jogger stroller is easier to maneuver than a traditional stroller.

TOWN HALL ARTS CENTER   AGES 7+

2450 W. Main St.
Littleton, CO 80120   303-794-2787
www.townhallartscenter.com

Hours: Vary - call or visit their website

Cost: Varies

What to Expect: A performing arts center showing quality live family entertainment in theatre, music and dance. Shows at the Children's Theatre are an affordable option. Children's Summer Theatre Workshops are designed for children ages 7-18. The Cultural Classroom gives students K-6 a positive theatre experience with all the magic that learning offers!

Notes/Tips: Free parking is available near the entrance. This is a great way to introduce your little actors and dancers to the performing arts.

TUBING AT COPPER MTN. $$$ AGES 5+

East Village at the base of Super Bee Lift
Copper, CO 80443   866-416-9874
www.coppercolorado.com Click on Plan & Buy, Coca-Cola Tubing Hill
(Access to this website is not available in the off-season.)

Hours: Vary – Call or visit the website

Cost: Kids under 13 yrs. $20/hour, Adults and Kids 13+ yrs. $24/hour, Additional hour $18, (Kids must be 36" tall)

What to Expect: A lift will carry you up beyond 9,712 feet where you will begin your spine-tingling ride down the snow chute. You and your family will want to experience this fun time and time again.

Notes/Tips: To purchase tickets, call number above or buy online. Riders can choose to go down the hill individually or in pairs. The tubing season is usually December thru April.

TUBING AT KEYSTONE
(Adventure Point) $$$ AGES 5+

At Dercum Mountain
Official Keystone Resort Wear in River Run Village
US Highway 6
Keystone, CO 80435   970-496-4386
http://keystone.snow.com/info/winter.asp
(Access to this website is not available in the off-season.)

Hours: Daily 12 pm to 4 pm, late November – Mid April. One hour sessions every half hour - weather permitting.

Cost: $25 per person and kids must be 42" tall.

What to Expect: To be lifted to the top of Dercum Mountain.   You will gasp at Colorado's beauty and snow-capped mountains. As you climb inside your inflatable ring, your anticipation of an exhilarating ride will soon become a reality as you experience winter fun at its best.

Notes/Tips: Reservations are necessary due to its fun factor.   Tickets can be purchased by calling the number above. Cancellation requires 24 hour notice. Check in 30 minutes prior to your reservation at the Official Resort Wear Store.   Day of tickets can be purchased at the official Keystone Resort Wear Store. Weather changes quickly and the temperature is usually more than ten degrees colder at the top. Parking is available in River Run Village for free or in pay lots Hunki Dori and Gold Bug.

TUBING AT KEYSTONE
(Old Fashioned Family) $$ AGES 3+

Keystone Nordic Center
Golf Club House at River Golf Course
Elk Drive off of US Highway 6
Keystone, CO 80435   970-496-4275
http://keystone.snow.com/info/winter.asp
(Access to this website is not available in the off-season.)

Hours: Daily 9 am to 4:30 pm, late November – Mid April – Weather permitting

Cost: $15/tube/hr.

What to Expect: A medium size hill that is designed for younger members of the family. This activity is guaranteed to tire the family because tubers are required to walk up and carry their tubes.

Notes/Tips: Tube availability is based on first-come, first-serve basis. No personal sleds or tubes are allowed. Tickets can be purchased by calling the number above. See website for great information on recommended attire. Parking is free.

UNITED STATES MINT ☺   AGES ALL

320 W. Colfax Ave.
Denver, CO 80204   *303-405-4761
www.usmint.gov Click on tours/Denver

Hours: Mon. – Fri. 8 am to 2 pm. Closed on federal holidays

Cost: Free

What to Expect: Approximately an hour long tour displaying the design and production of U.S. coins.

Notes/Tips: Plan to make reservations several weeks in advance online or by visiting the reservations booth. *Call 24 hours in advance to confirm your reservation. Arrive 15 minutes early. Late arrivals will not be admitted. No cell phones, cameras, smoking, drinking, eating, diaper bags or strollers are allowed. You may bring a palm sized wallet. No storage is available at the Mint for personal belongings. Allow extra time for parking. Interesting facts can be found on their website. This is a learning experience that both you and your child will remember.

WATER WORLD $$$$ 🎁

AGES 2+

1800 W. 89th Ave.
Federal Heights, CO 80260

303-427-7873

www.waterworldcolorado.com

Hours: Daily 10 am to 6 pm, Memorial Day to Labor Day, weather permitting. Hours are reduced beginning mid-August.

Cost: Kids (under 40") **free**, Kids (40"-47") $29.99, General Admission (48"+) $34.99, Seniors (60+) $5.99. Tickets are much less from 1:45 pm to 6 pm.   Discounts apply to residents of Hyland Hills and Westminster with recreation identification card.   Personal checks not accepted. Spectators have to pay full admission.

What to Expect: A family water park, which includes over 35 attractions, family tube rides, water slides and great toddler swim areas. Water World was recently named by the Travel Channel as one of the best water parks in America. The water is heated to around 77-80 degrees depending on the weather.

Notes/Tips: You can save time and money by purchasing tickets online if you don't have a coupon. Check the website for a list of merchants offering Water World coupons. The park is very large, so it is a good idea to choose a meeting place in case someone gets lost. We strongly recommend water shoes and downloading the guest information guide before you leave. You might want to check out the thrill rating on the website for each ride before you leave. If nothing else, you will know the rides that you want to watch from a far. Parking is free and picnics are allowed. All beverages must be factory sealed.

The early bird gets the lawn chairs and/or a spot in the shade. We highly recommend a chair and some shade. Lockers are available for your valuables.

Life jackets are free with a refundable deposit. You can rent your own tube for an additional $6 to avoid standing in line. The extra fee can be worth it on really busy days.

THE WILDLIFE EXPERIENCE $ 🎁   AGES 1+

10035 S. Peoria
Parker, CO 80134   720-488-3300
www.thewildlifeexperience.org   info@twexp.org

Hours: Tues. - Sun., 9 am to 5 pm and holidays that fall on a Monday.

Cost: (General Admission) Kids under 3 **free**, Kids 3-12 yrs. $6, Adults 13-64 yrs. $10, Seniors (65+) $9. See website for additional theater costs.

What to Expect: Educational and hands on exhibits such as: environmental conservation, Africa's terrain and studying wildlife remains. See website for current films and upcoming exhibits. The little ones up to age five can participate in crafts and try on animal costumes.

Notes/Tips: Enjoy the outdoor picnic area, nature trail, and café while you are there. If you are feeling brave, check out the live snake. Otherwise, watch the staff feed the fish in the aquarium. Ask for times before you arrive. Strollers, lockers and wheelchairs rentals are available. Parking is free.

WINGS OVER THE ROCKIES
AIR & SPACE MUSEUM $ 🎁   AGES ALL

7711 E. Academy Blvd.
Denver, CO 80230   303-360-5360
www.wingsmuseum.org

Hours: Mon. – Sat. 10 am to 5 pm, Sun. 12 pm to 5 pm

Cost: Kids under 4 **free**, Kids 4-12 yrs. $6, Adults $9, Seniors (65+) $8

What to Expect: An exciting journey through the evolution of aviation history with over three dozen extraordinary airplanes and space vehicles.

64

Notes/Tips: On the second Saturday of each month from 10:00 am to 2:00 pm, families can enjoy cockpit demonstration day. This means you sitting in the cockpit! Also on demo day, kids are allowed to ride in the pedal pusher airplanes. This will extend your visit and enable adults some extra time to see the museum's many exhibits. Summer camps are available for 3rd to 6th graders.

YOUNG AMERICANS CENTER
FOR FINANCIAL EDUCATION ☺   AGES 4-21

3550 E. First Ave.
Denver, CO 80206   303-321-2265
www.yacenter.org

Hours: Mon. – Fri. 10 am to 5 pm, Sat. 10 am to 3 pm

Cost: Free

What to Expect: A unique banking experience specifically designed for kids all the way up to the age 21. This special bank offers financial education, banking and a domestic and international town. A variety of summer camps, like starting a business and how to be a young entrepreneur are available for kids to learn about the financial world. Bank tellers will help your child open a savings account and deposit all the coins from piggy banks. Other bank services include: savings accounts, checking accounts, loans, CDs, credit, debit and ATM cards, all for kids.

Notes/Tips: AmeriTowne is for 5th and 6th graders on a field trip. International Towne is designed for 6th, 7th and 8th graders to learn about different economies in the world. The towns are also offered at the summer camps.

This kid-friendly bank offers classes to teach kids all about money, like opening a savings and checking account, applying for a credit card, and international currency exchange. The **free** Money Matters classes are on

Saturdays and fill up fast. At the end of the class, the students receive $5 bonus bucks to deposit into their savings account. Ten dollars and your child's social security card is all they need to open a savings account. Loans for the young financial experts-to-be can be applied for to buy bikes, video game systems and even a car.

FREE OR ALMOST FREE KIDS MEALS

RESTAURANTS

Below you will find a list of restaurants where kids eat **free** or almost **free**. Normally, adults must purchase a meal and one child eats **free**. Keep in mind that specials change frequently. Please call before visiting to ensure the special is still valid and to learn about any specific purchase requirements.

MONDAY

BROTHER'S BBQ
www.brothers-bbq.com

565 US Highway 287
Broomfield, CO 80020   303-635-2424
        Kids eat **free** all day

105 Wadsworth Blvd., Unit E
Lakewood, CO 80226   303-232-3422
        Kids eat **free** all day

BUFFALO WILD WINGS
www.buffalowildwings.com

8350 W. 80th Ave.
Arvada, CO 80005   303-424-2999
        Kids eat for $.99 all day

8255 S. Chester St., Ste. 200
Centennial, CO 80112   303-768-9464
        Kids eat for $.99 all day

5138 S. Wadsworth Blvd.
Lakewood, CO 80123   303-978-9424
        Kids eat for $1.99 all day

415 S. Wadsworth Blvd.
Lakewood, CO 80226   720-963-9464
        Kids eat for $1.99 all day

BUFFALO WILD WINGS (Cont'd.)

2303 Clover Basin Dr.
Longmont, CO 80503   303-485-9464
    Kids eat for $1.99 all day

404 Marshall Rd.
Superior, CO 80027   303-497-9464
    Kids eat for $1.99 all day

10090 Grant St.
Thornton, CO 80229   720-929-9464
    Kids eat for $1.99 all day

10436 Town Center Dr., Ste. 100
Westminster, CO 80021   303-465-2999
    Kids eat for $1.99 all day

CHICK-FIL-A
www.chick-fil-a.com

2580 Coalton Rd.
Broomfield, CO 80027   303-410-7050
  Kids eat **free** from 5 pm to 8 pm on the last
Monday of the Month if kids dress up for theme night.
    See website for details.

16670 Washington St.
Thornton, CO 80023   303-450-3322
  Kids eat **free** from 5 pm to 8 pm on the last
Monday of the Month if kids dress up for theme night.
    See website for details.

CINZZETTI'S
http://cinzzettis.com

281 W. 104th Ave.
Northglenn, CO 80234   303-451-7300
  Kids eat **free** from 5 pm to 9 pm

MONDAY

DENNY'S
www.dennys.com

275 W. Hampden Ave.
Englewood, CO 80110   303-761-6155
      Kids eat **free** from 4 pm to 10 pm

GUNTHER TOODY'S
www.gunthertoodys.com

7355 Ralston Rd.
Arvada, CO 80002   303-422-1954
      Kids eat **free** 11 am to close

4500 E. Alameda Ave.
Glendale, CO 80246   303-399-1959
      Kids eat **free** 11 am to close

9220 E. Arapahoe Rd.
Greenwood Village, CO 80112   303-799-1958
      Kids eat **free** 11 am to close

16755 N. Washington St.
Thornton, CO 80602   303-451-1950
      Kids eat **free** 11 am to close

IHOP
www.ihop.com

5280 Wadsworth Bypass, Bldg. P
Arvada, CO 80002   303-425-1134
      Kids eat **free** from 4 pm to 10 pm

5820 S. Parker Rd.
Aurora, CO 80015   303-400-4467
      Kids eat **free** from 3 pm to 9 pm

1675 28th St.
Boulder, CO 80301   303-444-2115
      Kids eat **free** from 3 pm to 9 pm

MONDAY

IHOP (Cont'd.)

575 Genoa Way
Castle Rock, CO 80104   303-814-2246
      Kids eat **free** from 4 pm to 9 pm

3730 Quebec St.
Denver, CO 80207   303-399-4646
      Kids eat **free** from 4 pm to 10 pm

3100 S. Sheridan Blvd.
Denver, CO 80227   303-936-6473
      Kids eat **free** from 2 pm to close

7017 S. Clinton St.
Englewood, CO 80112   303-790-1818
      Kids eat **free** from 3 pm to 9 pm

800 Englewood Pkwy.
Englewood, CO 80110   303-761-4467
      Kids eat **free** after 2 pm

9565 S. University Blvd.
Highlands Ranch, CO 80126   720-344-7383
      Kids eat **free** from 4 pm to 10 pm

7733 W. Long Dr.
Littleton, CO 80123   303-904-9609
      Kids eat **free** from 4 pm to 10 pm

12634 W. Indore Pl.
Littleton, CO 80127   720-922-8804
      Kids eat **free** from 4 pm to 10 pm

11355 S. Parker Rd.
Parker, CO 80134   720-851-8121
      Kids eat **free** from 3 pm to 10 pm

4730 W. 120th Ave.
Westminster, CO 80020   303-410-8900
      Kids eat **free** from 4 pm to 10 pm

MONDAY

RIO GRANDE MEXICAN RESTAURANT
http://riograndemexican.com/

9535 Park Meadows Dr.
Lone Tree, CO 80124   303-799-4999
      Kids eat **free** all day

SOUPER SALAD
www.soupersalad.com

12293 A E. Iliff Ave.
Aurora, CO 80014   303-751-1345
      Kids ages 0-3 **free**, Kids ages 4-10 $3.49

7939 E. Arapahoe Ste. 190
Greenwood Village, CO 80112   303-779-4493
      Kids ages 0-3 **free,** Kids ages 4-10 $3.49

7650 Virginia Ave. Ste. #A
Lakewood, CO 80226   303-989-2202
      Kids ages 0-3 **free,** Kids ages 4-10 $3.49

8936 W. Bowles Ave.
Littleton, CO 80123   303-932-2080
      Kids ages 0-3 **free**, Kids ages 4-10 $1.99

11930 Washington St.
Northglenn, CO 80233   720-872-0331
      Kids ages 0-3 **free**, Kids ages 4-10 $3.79

7685 W. 88th Ave.
Westminster, CO 80005   303-421-0203
      Kids ages 0-3 **free**, Kids ages 4-10 $3.49

MONDAY

TUESDAY

ATLANTA BREAD
www.atlantabread.com

14262 E. Cedar Ave.
Aurora, CO 80012   303-341-6200
> Kids eat **free** after 4 pm

7740 W. Alameda Ave. Unit E
Lakewood, CO 80226   303-991-4400
> Kids eat **free** 5:30 pm to 7 pm

351 W. 104th Ave.
Northglenn, CO 80234   303-452-8222
> Kids eat **free** after 4 pm

BLACK EYED PEA
www.blackeyedpeacolorado.com

850 New Memphis Ct.
Castle Rock, CO 80104   303-663-1105
> Kids eat **free** all day

1470 S. Colorado Blvd.
Denver, CO 80222   303-691-3470
> Kids eat **free** after 5 pm

5180 S. Broadway
Englewood, CO 80113   303-788-1350
> Kids eat **free** all day

94 Wadsworth Blvd.
Lakewood, CO 80226   303-238-5810
> Kids eat **free** after 5 pm

211 W. 104th Ave.
Northglenn, CO 80234   303-450-6434
> Kids eat **free** all day

TUESDAY

BROTHER'S BBQ
www.brothers-bbq.com

105 Wadsworth Blvd., Unit E
Lakewood, CO 80226   303-232-3422
          Kids eat **free** all day

2589 S. Lewis Way
Lakewood, CO 80227   303-989-9595
          Kids eat **free** all day

CHAMPPS
www.champps.com

7301 S. Santa Fe Dr.
Littleton, CO 80120   303-707-0333
          Kids eat **free** all day

8325 Park Meadows Center Dr.
Lone Tree, CO 80124   303-799-1333
          Kids eat **free** all day

CHICK-FIL-A
www.chick-fil-a.com

14200 E. Alameda Ave.
Aurora, CO 80012   303-364-8601
          Kids eat **free** from 5 pm to 8 pm

10280 Federal Blvd.
Federal Heights, CO 80260   720-887-1676
          Kids eat **free** from 5 pm to 8 pm

1301 E. 120th Ave.
Thornton, CO 80233   720-889-1471
          Kids eat **free** from 5 pm to 8 pm

TUESDAY

CINZZETTI'S
http://cinzzettis.com

281 W. 104th Ave.
Northglenn, CO 80234   303-451-7300
    Kids eat **free** from 5 pm to 9 pm

DENNY'S
www.dennys.com

1505 S. Havana
Aurora, CO 80012   303-750-6425
    Kids eat **free** from 4 pm to 10 pm

900 W. Alameda Ave.
Denver, CO 80223   303-744-7344
    Kids eat **free** from 4 pm to 10 pm

1605 N.W. Federal Blvd.
Denver, CO 80204   303-893-2627
    Kids eat **free** from 4 pm to 10 pm

275 W. Hampden Ave.
Englewood, CO 80110   303-761-6155
    Kids eat **free** from 4 pm to 10 pm

3580 S. Wadsworth Blvd.
Lakewood, CO 80235   303-988-2762
    Kids eat **free** from 4 pm to 10 pm

TUESDAY

FAZOLI'S
www.fazolis.com

5480 Wadsworth Bypass
Arvada, CO 80003   303-423-8189
    Kids eat for .99 from 5 pm to 8 pm

1012 S. Abilene
Aurora, CO 80012   303-745-6336
    Kids eat for .99 from 5 pm to 8 pm

8260 S. Quebec St.
Centennial, CO 80112   720-214-5502
    Kids eat for .99 from all day

111 W. Mineral Ave.
Littleton, CO 80120   303-738-0371
    Kids eat for .99 from 5 pm to 8 pm

460 E. 120th Ave.
Northglenn, CO 80233   303-452-9221
    Kids eat for .99 from 5 pm to 8 pm

IHOP
www.ihop.com

5280 Wadsworth Bypass, Bldg. P
Arvada, CO 80002   303-425-1134
    Kids eat **free** from 4 pm to 10 pm

5820 S. Parker Rd.
Aurora, CO 80015   303-400-4467
    Kids eat **free** from 3 pm to 9 pm

1675 28th St.
Boulder, CO 80301   303-444-2115
    Kids eat **free** from 3 pm to 9 pm

575 Genoa Way
Castle Rock, CO 80104   303-814-2246
    Kids eat **free** from 4 pm to 9 pm

IHOP (Cont'd.)

3730 Quebec St.
Denver, CO 80207   303-399-4646
     Kids eat **free** from 4 pm to 10 pm

3100 S. Sheridan Blvd.
Denver, CO 80227   303-936-6473
     Kids eat **free** from 2 pm to close

7017 S. Clinton St.
Englewood, CO 80112   303-790-1818
     Kids eat **free** from 3 pm to 9 pm

800 Englewood Pkwy.
Englewood, CO 80110   303-761-4467
     Kids eat **free** after 2 pm

9565 S. University Blvd.
Highlands Ranch, CO 80126   720-344-7383
     Kids eat **free** from 4 pm to 10 pm

7733 W. Long Dr.
Littleton, CO 80123   303-904-9609
     Kids eat **free** from 4 pm to 10 pm

12634 W. Indore Pl.
Littleton, CO 80127   720-922-8804
     Kids eat **free** from 4 pm to 10 pm

11355 S. Parker Rd.
Parker, CO 80134   720-851-8121
     Kids eat **free** from 3 pm to 10 pm

4730 W. 120th Ave.
Westminster, CO 80020   303-410-8900
     Kids eat **free** from 4 pm to 10 pm

TUESDAY

LONE STAR STEAKHOUSE
www.lonestarsteakhouse.com

305 Pavilions Pl.
Brighton, CO 80601 303-655-9433
   Kids eat **free** all day

11905 W. 6th Ave.
Golden, CO 80401 303-237-5727
   Kids eat **free** all day

4817 S. Wadsworth Blvd.
Littleton, CO 80123 303-932-1718
   Kids eat **free** all day

237 E. 120th Ave.
Thornton, CO 80233 303-252-0770
   Kids eat **free** all day

THE MELTING POT
www.meltingpot.com

2707 W. Main St.
Littleton, CO 80120 303-794-5666
   Kids eat **free** from 5 pm to 7 pm

732 Main St.
Louisville, CO 80027 303-666-7777
   Kids eat **free** from 5 pm to 7 pm

PERKINS
www.perkinsrestaurants.com

8691 Sheridan Blvd.
Arvada, CO 80003 303-427-5740
   Kids eat **free** from 4 pm to 10 pm

1995 S. Colorado Blvd.
Denver, CO 80222 303-757-7155
   Kids eat **free** from 4 pm to 10 pm

TUESDAY

PERKINS (Cont'd.)

1495 Simms St.
Golden, CO 80401   303-237-1339
      Kids eat **free** from 4 pm to 10 pm

3244 S. Wadsworth Blvd.
Lakewood, CO 80227   303-989-7919
      Kids eat **free** from 4 pm to 10 pm

2051 N. Main St.
Longmont, CO 80501   303-772-1410
      Kids eat **free** all day

12015 Melody Dr.
Westminster, CO 80030   303-452-6200
      Kids eat **free** from 4 pm to 10 pm

SOUPER SALAD
www.soupersalad.com

12293 A E. Iliff Ave.
Aurora, CO 80014   303-751-1345
    Kids ages 0-3 **free**, Kids ages 4-10 $3.49

7939 E. Arapahoe Ste. 190
Greenwood Village, CO 80112   303-779-4493
    Kids ages 0-3 **free,** Kids ages 4-10 $3.49

7650 Virginia Ave. Ste. #A
Lakewood, CO 80226   303-989-2202
    Kids ages 0-3 **free,** Kids ages 4-10 $3.49

8936 W. Bowles Ave.
Littleton, CO 80123   303-932-2080
    Kids ages 0-3 **free**, Kids ages 4-10 $3.49

TUESDAY

11930 Washington St.
Northglenn, CO 80233   720-872-0331
    Kids ages 0-3 **free**, Kids ages 4-10 $3.79

7685 W. 88th Ave.
Westminster, CO 80005   303-421-0203
    Kids ages 0-3 **free**, Kids ages 4-10 $3.49

TUESDAY

APPLEBEE'S
www.applebees.com

5265 Wadsworth Bypass
Arvada, CO 80002   303-421-1032
        Kids eat for .99 all day

14091 E. Iliff Ave.
Aurora, CO 80014   303-745-9897
        Kids eat for .99 all day

1906 S. 28th St.
Boulder, CO 80301   303-442-8813
        Kids eat for .99 all day

922 S. 4th Ave.
Brighton, CO 80601   720-685-1095
        Kids eat for .99 all day

6405 W. 120th Ave.
Broomfield, CO 80020   303-466-3848
        Kids eat for .99 all day

1078 Allen St.
Castle Rock, CO 80104   303-814-0230
        Kids eat for .99 all day

8292 S. University Blvd.
Centennial, CO 80122   303-770-3383
        Kids eat for .99 all day

410 S. Colorado Blvd.
Glendale, CO 80246   303-333-0808
        Kids eat for .99 all day

5250 S. Wadsworth Blvd.
Lakewood, CO 80123   303-933-2230
        Kids eat for .99 all day

10625 W. Colfax Ave.
Lakewood, CO 80226   303-462-1782
        Kids eat for .99 all day

100 W. 104th Ave.
Northglenn, CO 80234   303-252-7422
        Kids eat for .99 all day

297 E. 120th Ave.
Thornton, CO 80233   303-451-1414
        Kids eat for .99 all day

9010 N. Wadsworth Pkwy.
Westminster, CO 80021   303-431-9022
        Kids eat for .99 all day

DENNY'S
www.dennys.com

275 W. Hampden Ave.
Englewood, CO 80110   303-761-6155
        Kids eat **free** from 4 pm to 10 pm

IHOP
www.ihop.com

5280 Wadsworth Bypass, Bldg. P
Arvada, CO 80002   303-425-1134
        Kids eat **free** from 4 pm to 10 pm

5820 S. Parker Rd.
Aurora, CO 80015   303-400-4467
        Kids eat **free** from 3 pm to 9 pm

1675 28th St.
Boulder, CO 80301   303-444-2115
        Kids eat **free** from 3 pm to 9 pm

WEDNESDAY

IHOP (Cont'd.)

575 Genoa Way
Castle Rock, CO 80104   303-814-2246
          Kids eat **free** from 4 pm to 9 pm

3730 Quebec St.
Denver, CO 80207   303-399-4646
          Kids eat **free** from 4 pm to 10 pm

3100 S. Sheridan Blvd.
Denver, CO 80227   303-936-6473
          Kids eat **free** from 2 pm to close

7017 S. Clinton St.
Englewood, CO 80112   303-790-1818
          Kids eat **free** from 3 pm to 9 pm

800 Englewood Pkwy.
Englewood, CO 80110   303-761-4467
          Kids eat **free** after 2 pm

9565 S. University Blvd.
Highlands Ranch, CO 80126   720-344-7383
          Kids eat **free** from 4 pm to 10 pm

7733 W. Long Dr.
Littleton, CO 80123   303-904-9609
          Kids eat **free** from 4 pm to 10 pm

12634 W. Indore Pl.
Littleton, CO 80127   720-922-8804
          Kids eat **free** from 4 pm to 10 pm

11355 S. Parker Rd.
Parker, CO 80134   720-851-8121
          Kids eat **free** from 3 pm to 10 pm

4730 W. 120th Ave.
Westminster, CO 80020   303-410-8900
          Kids eat **free** from 4 pm to 10 pm

WEDNESDAY

LODO'S
www.lodosbarandgrill.com

3053 W. 104th Ave.
Westminster, CO 80031   303-635-8025
    Kids eat **free** from 6 pm to 9 pm

SOUPER SALAD
www.soupersalad.com

12293 A E. Iliff Ave.
Aurora, CO 80014   303-751-1345
    Kids ages 0-3 **free**, Kids ages 4-10 $3.49

7939 E. Arapahoe Ste. 190
Greenwood Village, CO 80112   303-779-4493
    Kids ages 0-3 **free,** Kids ages 4-10 $3.49

7650 Virginia Ave. Ste. #A
Lakewood, CO 80226   303-989-2202
    Kids ages 0-3 **free,** Kids ages 4-10 $3.49

8936 W. Bowles Ave.
Littleton, CO 80123   303-932-2080
    Kids ages 0-3 **free**, Kids ages 4-10 $3.49

11930 Washington St.
Northglenn, CO 80233   720-872-0331
    Kids ages 0-3 **free**, Kids ages 4-10 $3.79

7685 W. 88th Ave.
Westminster, CO 80005   303-421-0203
    Kids ages 0-3 **free**, Kids ages 4-10 $3.49

WEDNESDAY

WOODY'S WOOD-FIRED TAVERN
www.woodyswoodfiredtavern.com

7995 Sheridan Blvd.
Arvada, CO 80003   303-650-5500
>> Kids eat **free** from 4 pm to 9 pm

7095 E. Evans Ave.
Denver, CO 80224   303-757-4200
>> Kids eat **free** from 4 pm to 9 pm

WEDNESDAY

THURSDAY

C.B. & POTTS
www.cbpotts.com

555 Zang St.
Broomfield, CO 80020   720-887-3383
           Kids eat for $1 all day

6575 S. Greenwood Plaza Blvd.
Englewood, CO 80111   303-770-1982
           Kids eat for $1 all day

43 W. Centennial Blvd.
Highlands Ranch, CO 80126   720-344-1200
           Kids eat for $1 all day

1257 W. 120th Ave.
Westminster, CO 80234   303-451-5767
           Kids eat for $1 all day

DENNY'S
www.dennys.com

275 W. Hampden Ave.
Englewood, CO 80110   303-761-6155
       Kids eat **free** from 4 pm to 10 pm

IHOP
www.ihop.com

5280 Wadsworth Bypass, Bldg. P
Arvada, CO 80002   303-425-1134
       Kids eat **free** from 4 pm to 10 pm

5820 S. Parker Rd.
Aurora, CO 80015   303-400-4467
       Kids eat **free** from 3 pm to 9 pm

1675 28th St.
Boulder, CO 80301   303-444-2115
       Kids eat **free** from 3 pm to 9 pm

IHOP (Cont'd.)

575 Genoa Way
Castle Rock, CO 80104   303-814-2246
Kids eat **free** from 4 pm to 9 pm

3730 Quebec St.
Denver, CO 80207   303-399-4646
Kids eat **free** from 4 pm to 10 pm

3100 S. Sheridan Blvd.
Denver, CO 80227   303-936-6473
Kids eat **free** from 2 pm to close

7017 S. Clinton St.
Englewood, CO 80112   303-790-1818
Kids eat **free** from 3 pm to 9 pm

800 Englewood Pkwy.
Englewood, CO 80110   303-761-4467
Kids eat **free** after 2 pm

9565 S. University Blvd.
Highlands Ranch, CO 80126   720-344-7383
Kids eat **free** from 4 pm to 10 pm

7733 W. Long Dr.
Littleton, CO 80123   303-904-9609
Kids eat **free** from 4 pm to 10 pm

12634 W. Indore Pl.
Littleton, CO 80127   720-922-8804
Kids eat **free** from 4 pm to 10 pm

11355 S. Parker Rd.
Parker, CO 80134   720-851-8121
Kids eat **free** from 3 pm to 10 pm

4730 W. 120th Ave.
Westminster, CO 80020   303-410-8900
Kids eat **free** from 4 pm to 10 pm

THURSDAY

SOUPER SALAD
www.soupersalad.com

12293 A E. Iliff Ave.
Aurora, CO 80014   303-751-1345
        Kids ages 0-3 **free**, Kids ages 4-10 $3.49

7939 E. Arapahoe Ste. 190
Greenwood Village, CO 80112   303-779-4493
        Kids ages 0-3 **free,** Kids ages 4-10 $3.49

7650 Virginia Ave. Ste. #A
Lakewood, CO 80226   303-989-2202
        Kids ages 0-3 **free,** Kids ages 4-10 $3.49

8936 W. Bowles Ave.
Littleton, CO 80123   303-932-2080
        Kids ages 0-3 **free**, Kids ages 4-10 $3.49

11930 Washington St.
Northglenn, CO 80233   720-872-0331
        Kids ages 0-3 **free**, Kids ages 4-10 $3.79

7685 W. 88th Ave.
Westminster, CO 80005   303-421-0203
        Kids ages 0-3 **free**, Kids ages 4-10 $3.49

THURSDAY

FRIDAY

DENNY'S
www.dennys.com

275 W. Hampden Ave.
Englewood, CO 80110   303-761-6155
>Kids eat **free** from 4 pm to 10 pm

IHOP
www.ihop.com

5280 Wadsworth Bypass, Bldg. P
Arvada, CO 80002   303-425-1134
>Kids eat **free** from 4 pm to 10 pm

5820 S. Parker Rd.
Aurora, CO 80015   303-400-4467
>Kids eat **free** from 3 pm to 9 pm

1675 28th St.
Boulder, CO 80301   303-444-2115
>Kids eat **free** from 3 pm to 9 pm

575 Genoa Way
Castle Rock, CO 80104   303-814-2246
>Kids eat **free** from 4 pm to 9 pm

3730 Quebec St.
Denver, CO 80207   303-399-4646
>Kids eat **free** from 4 pm to 10 pm

3100 S. Sheridan Blvd.
Denver, CO 80227   303-936-6473
>Kids eat **free** from 2 pm to close

7017 S. Clinton St.
Englewood, CO 80112   303-790-1818
>Kids eat **free** from 3 pm to 9 pm

800 Englewood Pkwy.
Englewood, CO 80110   303-761-4467
        Kids eat **free** after 2 pm

9565 S. University Blvd.
Highlands Ranch, CO 80126   720-344-7383
        Kids eat **free** from 4 pm to 10 pm

7733 W. Long Dr.
Littleton, CO 80123   303-904-9609
        Kids eat **free** from 4 pm to 10 pm

12634 W. Indore Pl.
Littleton, CO 80127   720-922-8804
        Kids eat **free** from 4 pm to 10 pm

11355 S. Parker Rd.
Parker, CO 80134   720-851-8121
        Kids eat **free** from 3 pm to 10 pm

4730 W. 120th Ave.
Westminster, CO 80020   303-410-8900
        Kids eat **free** from 4 pm to 10 pm

SOUPER SALAD
www.soupersalad.com

12293 A E. Iliff Ave.
Aurora, CO 80014   303-751-1345
        Kids ages 0-3 **free**, Kids ages 4-10 $3.49

7939 E. Arapahoe Ste. 190
Greenwood Village, CO 80112   303-779-4493
        Kids ages 0-3 **free,** Kids ages 4-10 $3.49

7650 Virginia Ave. Ste. #A
Lakewood, CO 80226   303-989-2202
        Kids ages 0-3 **free,** Kids ages 4-10 $3.49

8936 W. Bowles Ave.
Littleton, CO 80123   303-932-2080
        Kids ages 0-3 **free,** Kids ages 4-10 $3.49

SOUPER SALAD (Cont'd.)

11930 Washington St.
Northglenn, CO 80233   720-872-0331
    Kids ages 0-3 **free**, Kids ages 4-10 $3.79

7685 W. 88th Ave.
Westminster, CO 80005   303-421-0203
    Kids ages 0-3 **free**, Kids ages 4-10 $3.49

FRIDAY

BONO'S BBQ
www.bonosbarbq.com

13881 E. Mississippi Ave.
Aurora, CO 80012   303-337-7427
> Kids eat **free** all day

9393 E. Dry Creek Rd.
Centennial, CO 80112   303-850-7427
> Kids eat **free** all day

DENNY'S
www.dennys.com

1505 S. Havana
Aurora, CO 80012   303-750-6425
> Kids eat **free** from 4 pm to 10 pm

900 W. Alameda Ave.
Denver, CO 80223   303-744-7344
> Kids eat **free** from 4 pm to 10 pm

1605 N.W. Federal Blvd.
Denver, CO 80204   303-893-2627
> Kids eat **free** from 4 pm to 10 pm

275 W. Hampden Ave.
Englewood, CO 80110   303-761-6155
> Kids eat **free** from 4 pm to 10 pm

3580 S. Wadsworth Blvd.
Lakewood, CO 80235   303-988-2762
> Kids eat **free** from 4 pm to 10 pm

SATURDAY

IHOP
www.ihop.com

5280 Wadsworth Bypass, Bldg. P
Arvada, CO 80002   303-425-1134
>   Kids eat **free** from 4 pm to 10 pm

575 Genoa Way
Castle Rock, CO 80104   303-814-2246
>   Kids eat **free** from 4 pm to 9 pm

3730 Quebec St.
Denver, CO 80207   303-399-4646
>   Kids eat **free** from 4 pm to 10 pm

3100 S. Sheridan Blvd.
Denver, CO 80227   303-936-6473
>   Kids eat **free** all day

7017 S. Clinton St.
Englewood, CO 80112   303-790-1818
>   Kids eat **free** from 3 pm to 9 pm

800 Englewood Pkwy.
Englewood, CO 80110   303-761-4467
>   Kids eat **free** all day

9565 S. University Blvd.
Highlands Ranch, CO 80126   720-344-7383
>   Kids eat **free** from 4 pm to 10 pm

7733 W. Long Dr.
Littleton, CO 80123   303-904-9609
>   Kids eat **free** from 4 pm to 10 pm

12634 W. Indore Pl.
Littleton, CO 80127   720-922-8804
>   Kids eat **free** from 4 pm to 10 pm

4730 W. 120th Ave.
Westminster, CO 80020   303-410-8900
>   Kids eat **free** from 4 pm to 10 pm

LODO'S
www.lodosbarandgrill.com

1946 Market St.
Denver, CO 80202 303-293-8555
        Kids eat for $2.99 all day

3053 W. 104th Ave.
Westminster, CO 80031 303-635-8025
        Kids eat for $2.99 all day

PERKINS
www.perkinsrestaurants.com

8691 Sheridan Blvd.
Arvada, CO 80003 303-427-5740
        Kids eat **free** from 4 pm to 10 pm

1995 S. Colorado Blvd.
Denver, CO 80222 303-757-7155
        Kids eat **free** from 4 pm to 10 pm

1495 Simms St.
Golden, CO 80401 303-237-1339
        Kids eat **free** from 4 pm to 10 pm

3244 S. Wadsworth Blvd.
Lakewood, CO 80227 303-989-7919
        Kids eat **free** from 4 pm to 10 pm

12015 Melody Dr.
Westminster, CO 80030 303-452-6200
        Kids eat **free** from 4 pm to 10 pm

SATURDAY

PIZZERIA UNO
www.unos.com

16375 E. 40th Ave.
Denver, CO 80239   303-371-1555
Kids eat **free** all day

SOUPER SALAD
www.soupersalad.com

12293 A E. Iliff Ave.
Aurora, CO 80014   303-751-1345
Kids ages 0-3 **free**, Kids ages 4-10 $3.49

7939 E. Arapahoe Ste. 190
Greenwood Village, CO 80112   303-779-4493
Kids ages 0-3 **free,** Kids ages 4-10 $3.49

7650 Virginia Ave. Ste. #A
Lakewood, CO 80226   303-989-2202
Kids ages 0-3 **free,** Kids ages 4-10 $3.49

8936 W. Bowles Ave.
Littleton, CO 80123   303-932-2080
Kids ages 0-3 **free**, Kids ages 4-10 $3.49

11930 Washington St.
Northglenn, CO 80233   720-872-0331
Kids ages 0-3 **free**, Kids ages 4-10 $3.79

7685 W. 88th Ave.
Westminster, CO 80005   303-421-0203
Kids ages 0-3 **free**, Kids ages 4-10 $3.49

SATURDAY

SUNDAY

BONO'S BBQ
www.bonosbarbq.com

13881 E. Mississippi Ave.
Aurora, CO 80012   303-337-7427
       Kids eat **free** all day

9393 E. Dry Creek Rd.
Centennial, CO 80112   303-850-7427
       Kids eat **free** all day

DENNY'S
www.dennys.com

275 W. Hampden Ave.
Englewood, CO 80110   303-761-6155
       Kids eat **free** from 4 pm to 10 pm

IHOP
www.ihop.com

5280 Wadsworth Bypass, Bldg. P
Arvada, CO 80002   303-425-1134
       Kids eat **free** from 4 pm to 10 pm

575 Genoa Way
Castle Rock, CO 80104   303-814-2246
       Kids eat **free** from 4 pm to 9 pm

3730 Quebec St.
Denver, CO 80207   303-399-4646
       Kids eat **free** from 4 pm to 10 pm

3100 S. Sheridan Blvd.
Denver, CO 80227   303-936-6473
       Kids eat **free** all day

7017 S. Clinton St.
Englewood, CO 80112   303-790-1818
       Kids eat **free** from 3 pm to 9 pm

IHOP (Cont'd.)

800 Englewood Pkwy.
Englewood, CO 80110   303-761-4467
            Kids eat **free** after 2 pm

9565 S. University Blvd.
Highlands Ranch, CO 80126   720-344-7383
            Kids eat **free** from 4 pm to 10 pm

7733 W. Long Dr.
Littleton, CO 80123   303-904-9609
            Kids eat **free** from 4 pm to 10 pm

12634 W. Indore Pl.
Littleton, CO 80127   720-922-8804
            Kids eat **free** from 4 pm to 10 pm

4730 W. 120th Ave.
Westminster, CO 80020   303-410-8900
            Kids eat **free** from 4 pm to 10 pm

LANDRY'S SEAFOOD HOUSE
www.landrysseafoodhouse.com
7209 S. Clinton St.
Englewood, CO 80112   303-792-0285
            Kids eat **free** all day

LANSDOWNE ARMS
http://www.lansdownearmsbistroandpub.com

9352 Dorchester St.
Highlands Ranch, CO 80129   303-346-8273
            Kids eat **free** from 11 am to 4 pm

LODO'S
www.lodosbarandgrill.com

1946 Market St.
Denver, CO 80202   303-293-8555
        Kids eat for $2.99 all day

3053 W. 104th Ave.
Westminster, CO 80031   303-635-8025
        Kids eat for $2.99 all day

THE MELTING POT
www.meltingpot.com

2707 W. Main St.
Littleton, CO 80120   303-794-5666
        Kids eat **free** from 3 pm to 4:45 pm

732 Main St.
Louisville, CO 80027   303-666-7777
        Kids eat **free** from 4 pm to 6 pm

SUNDAY

SOUPER SALAD
www.soupersalad.com

12293 A E. Iliff Ave.
Aurora, CO 80014   303-751-1345
    Kids ages 0-3 **free**, Kids ages 4-10 $2.49

7939 E. Arapahoe Ste. 190
Greenwood Village, CO 80112   303-779-4493
    Kids ages 0-3 **free**, Kids ages 4-10 $2.49

7650 Virginia Ave. Ste. #A
Lakewood, CO 80226   303-989-2202
    Kids ages 0-3 **free**, Kids ages 4-10 $2.49

8936 W. Bowles Ave.
Littleton, CO 80123   303-932-2080
    Kids ages 0-3 **free**, Kids ages 4-10 $2.49

11930 Washington St.
Northglenn, CO 80233   720-872-0331
    Kids ages 0-3 **free**, Kids ages 4-10 $2.49

7685 W. 88th Ave.
Westminster, CO 80005   303-421-0203
    Kids ages 0-3 **free**, Kids ages 4-10 $2.49

SUNDAY

FREE OR ALMOST FREE KID'S MEALS
BY RESTAURANT

Applebee's..W
Atlanta Bread ....T
Black Eyed Pea ....T
Bono's BBQ .... Sa, Su
Brother's BBQ ....M, T
Buffalo Wild Wings .... M
C.B. & Potts.. Th
Champps...T
Chick-Fil-A ....M, T
Cinzzetti's ....M, T
Denny's ....M, T, W, Th, F, Sa, Su
Fazoli's ....T
Gunther Toody's... M
IHOP ....M, T, W, Th, F, Sa, Su
Landry's Seafood House ....Su
Lansdowne Arms...Su
Lodo's ....W, Sa, Su
Lone Star Steakhouse...T
The Melting Pot... T, Su
Perkins .... T, Sa
Pizzeria Uno ....Sa
Rio Grande Mexican Restaurant .... M
Souper Salad.................................M, T, W, Th, F, Sa, Su
Woody's Wood-Fired Tavern ....W

INDEX

BIRTHDAY BASH DIRECTORY 🎁

American Mountaineering Museum 12
Arts on Fire 13
Brunswick Zone 15
Build-A-Bear Workshop 17
Butterfly Pavilion.. 18
The Children's Museum of Denver 20
Chuck E. Cheese's 21
Colorado Journey 24
Colorado Rockies... 25
County Line BMX.. 27
Denver Aquarium 28
Denver Firefighters Museum 30
Denver Museum of Nature & Science 30
Denver Puppet Theater 32
Dinosaur Ridge 33
Elitch Gardens 34
Fiske Planetarium and Science Center....................... 35
Fun City... 36
Hammond's Candies 39
Heritage Square.. 40
House of Bounce 41
Indoor Skydiving... 44
Jack & Jill Children's Salon................................. 45
Jo-Ann Fabric Superstore (Class Catalog) 46

Jungle Quest 47
Lollilocks Kids Salon 48
The Makery 50
Michaels.. 50
Monkey Bizness 51
Noah's Ark Animal Workshop 53
Peak Athletics Plus 53
Pirates Cove 54
Puppets and Things on Strings.................................... 55
Putting Edge Fun Center 56
Skate City 57
Snip-Its 58
String Beads.. 58
Water World 63
The Wildlife Experience 64
Wings Over the Rockies Air & Space Museum.................. 64

FAMILY FUN BY COST FOR ADULTS

☺ FREE
Air Force Academy 11
Colorado Avalanche Hockey Practice 23
Colorado State Capitol 26
County Line BMX 27
Denver Art Museum 28
Denver Museum of Nature & Science 30
Dinosaur Ridge 33
Governor's Residence at The Boettcher Mansion 39
Hammond's Candies 39
Home Depot (Kids Workshops) 40
Ice Skating at Copper 42
Littleton Historical Museum 48
Lowe's (Build and Grow Clinics) 49
Michaels (The Knack Kid's Program) 50
National Center for Atmospheric Research 52
National Oceanic Atmospheric Administration 52
Red Rocks Park 56
United States Mint 62
Young Americans Center for Financial Education 65

$ (UP TO $10)
AMC Theatres 12
American Mountaineering Museum 12
Brunswick Zone 15
Buffalo Bill Museum and Grave 16
Butterfly Pavilion 18
The Children's Museum Of Denver 20
Colorado Journey 24
Colorado Rockies 25
Denver Art Museum 28
Denver Firefighters Museum 30
Denver Puppet Theater 32

Fiske Planetarium and Science Center 35
House of Bounce 41
Ice Skating at Evergreen 43
The Molly Brown House Museum 51
Monkey Bizness 51
Pirates Cove 54
Putting Edge Fun Center 56
Skate City 57
String Beads 58
Tiny Town 59
The Wildlife Experience 64
Wings Over the Rockies Air & Space Museum 64

$$ ($10.01 TO $15)
Denver Aquarium 28
Denver Nuggets Basketball 31
Ice Skating At Keystone 43
Jungle Quest 47
Tubing at Keystone (Old Fashioned Family) 61

$$$ ($15.01 TO $25)
Build-A-Bear Workshop 17
Heritage Square 40
The Makery 50
Tubing at Copper Mtn. 60
Tubing at Keystone (Adventure Point) 61

$$$$ (MORE THAN $25)
Colorado Avalanche Hockey Game 23
Elitch Gardens 34
Indoor Skydiving 44
Jo-Ann Fabric Superstore (Class Catalog) 46
Noah's Ark Animal Workshop 53
Peak Athletics Plus 53
Snip-Its 58
Water World 63

COST VARIES

Arts on Fire 13
Cave of the Winds 18
Chuck E. Cheese's 21
Denver Center for the Performing Arts 29
Denver Museum of Nature & Science 30
Durango & Silverton Narrow Gauge Railroad 34
Fun City 36
Jack & Jill Children's Salon................................ 45
Lollilocks Kids Salon 48
Puppets and Things on Strings......................... 55
Royal Gorge Route Railroad 57
Town Hall Arts Center 60

ABOUT THE AUTHORS

JUSTINE M. DAVROS

I am a working mom, who has been married to a wonderful man for 16 years. We have a 12 year old son and he loves to stay busy. I have worked in the nonprofit industry for my entire career, serving youth and seniors. Like all moms, my favorite activity is spending time with my family.

My husband is a Paramedic Firefighter, which provides him with lots of wonderful one-to-one time with our son. I wanted them to have plenty of activities to do together, which would enrich their relationship. So one day, I skipped over to the bookstore to look for a directory of family fun activities. After an afternoon of endless page turning, I wasn't able to find that one great resource of fun to purchase.

CINDY NEAD

I am a domestic engineer. It's a fancy name for a stay-at-home mom. I live in Metro Denver with my husband of 16 years, my son and daughter. I enjoy the outdoors, hiking, biking and playing any sport with my kids.

Before starting a family, I held numerous positions within the financial services industry. When my youngest child was four, I realized that I was ready to take on a project, which was challenging, gratifying and gave me a sense of accomplishment. I could have gone back to work, but I needed a flexible schedule that didn't require a lengthy commute.

Although different paths led us to this point, Justine and I envisioned a great directory of fun activities. We met at a hockey rink during our sons' weekly practice and became friends right away. While comparing notes we had compiled about local attractions, we decided to combine our lists and publish Family Fun 411.

NOTES:

NOTES:

Feel free to contact us with questions, suggestions or updates.

Family Fun 411
PO Box 632166
Littleton, CO 80163

E-mail: **familyfun411@yahoo.com**

www.familyfun411.com
www.facebook.com/familyfun411
www.twitter.com/familyfun411